Even Hockey Players
READ

Boys, Literacy and Learn

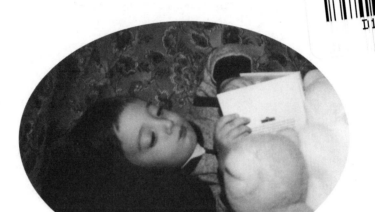

DAVID BOOTH

Pembroke Publishers Limited

For
Margaret Karr Lunan Keene
mother, aunt, and grandmother

© **2002 Pembroke Publishers**
538 Hood Road
Markham, Ontario, Canada L3R 3K9
www.pembrokepublishers.com

Distributed in the U.S. by Stenhouse Publishers
477 Congress Street
Portland, ME 04101

We acknowledge the financial support of the Government of Canada through the Book Publishing Industry Development Program (BPIDP) for our publishing activities.

National Library of Canada Cataloguing in Publication

Booth, David
    Even hockey players read : boys and reading / David Booth.

Includes index.
ISBN 1-55138-147-8

    1. Boys—Books and reading. 2. Boys—Education. I. Title.

LB1050.B66 2002   428.4'071   C2002-902882-5

Editor: Kate Revington
Cover Design: John Zehethofer
Cover Photo: Ajay Photographics
Typesetting: Jay Tee Graphics Ltd.

Printed and bound in Canada
9 8 7 6 5 4 3

Contents

Introduction: Into the Circle of Print

"Some of you reading this book have biological, adopted, foster or stepsons. Many of you have nephews and male cousins as well. Others of you may be teachers, counselors, coaches or Boy Scout leaders. All of you have boys in your life in some way. I am using the word son to encompass a number of relationships that we, as caring adults, have with boys and young men. In a society where some children are uncared for or neglected and in which competition and violence reign, none of our sons or daughters are safe, no matter how strong or independent or caring or nonsexist we raise our sons to be."

From Boys Will Be Men: Raising Our Sons for Courage, Caring and Community, *by Paul Kivel*

The title of this book comes from my son's childhood years, when I would try to promote more reading time at home. My son, Jay, would protest: "But I want to be a hockey player!" and I would retort, "Well, even hockey players read." And, of course, hockey players do read, and the variety of print materials that they handle would be similar to that of any group of men in similar organizations. But would their choices be the same as those of the members of a women's hockey team? While waiting for a plane in a fogged-in New York airport, I noticed a group of about 20 men dressed in Armani suits. Eventually I discovered that they were the New York Islanders hockey team. And what were they reading during the waiting time? I observed a range of print experiences: one chap was reading aloud to his group the newspaper report of last night's game; another was reading Ken Follett's latest espionage novel; one player was working his way through the *Financial Post*; one was exploring a computer magazine; another, a golf magazine; and so on. These were men who were reading, and their choices represented their interests, the resources available, and their life experiences at that time.

For me, this anecdote is useful in establishing a definition of what we can mean by the term *reading* in the lives of boys and men. Years ago the reading specialist Arn Bowers taught me to handle the question "Can you read?" by changing it to "What can you read?" Why? Because the nature of the *print text* being read affects so strongly the potential of the reader to make any significant meaning. What we read, whether as males or as females, is determined by our life experiences, sometimes by our constructed gender, by what we bring to the print, by our familiarity with the words and the style, by the expectations of the genre, by the social frames of the event, and, of course, by the content. Reading is a complex act for everyone, including hockey players.

During his final year in high school, my son Jay attended a residential hockey school, where the students practised the game from 6:30 a.m. until 10 a.m., and then had academic classes until 5 p.m. He considers it to be his best year in school: small classes, interested young teachers, classmates with similar goals, and the chance to do what he loved for much of the day. Although, as a teenager, I had friends who played hockey, this would not have been my activity of choice, but his experience there altered my understanding of the teaching/learning process for the rest of my life. Many boys (and some girls) see hockey as a life-fulfilling passion. How do they view reading and writing in and out of school? And does the question have much validity without adding, "*What* are they reading or writing?" Although the current interest in boys and reading is most probably fuelled by falling test scores, I want to look at the literacy world that my son finds himself in as a young adult male. I also want to examine the factors that appear to affect boys in our schools and homes in their development as readers and writers.

When I began researching material in this field, I was amazed at the quantity of available resources for parents and teachers, especially from the Internet. People are certainly concerned about males and literacy. Dozens of books have emerged in the last few years documenting issues in male culture and in raising and schooling boys. Some emphasize biological differences in males and females; others take a socio-constructivist approach; still others struggle for a culturally elitist model promoting literary wonders. Personally, I need to look at them all, to find directions for supporting parents and teachers and educational policy makers, but especially for helping youngsters themselves to begin taking control of their literacy lives, aware of their needs and interests as developing readers and writers.

I want to examine the issues pertaining to the literacy lives of boys, how they perceive themselves as readers, and how parents, teachers and peers influence their literacy development. The role of gender in reading success is complex, and I want to uncover many of the assumptions and stereotypes that parents and educators have about boys and how they handle the world of print text. For each issue I explore, I have included the voices of writers for young people, of authorities in these fields, and, most important, of boys and men that teachers in my preservice and graduate classes have interviewed and observed. There, male readers reveal their literacy challenges, struggles, tastes and values, and offer us insights into how we can support all children in their journey.

Consider the change in the texts we read today at home or work: books of every variety—softcover and hardback; thousands and thousands of magazines and comics available at the local newsstand; letters, bills, ads and pamphlets through the mailbox; electronic print of all sorts, from ones that fit in the palm to giant TV screens; memos, fact sheets, documents, e-mail and attachments. The definition of literacy has altered, as have the strategies necessary for reading texts.

If we believe that all children should have access to the literacy world, how will we ensure that boys, in particular, see themselves as readers who can handle the requirements of such a variety of texts? Non-readers tell us stories of punishment and pain, of no care and no touch, where books never metamorphosed into friendly objects, where worksheets and controlled readers dictated their eye movements and caused their reading hearts to beat irregularly. They drown in printer's ink.

The search for meaning is paramount in all our lives. The daughter of a stroke victim was attempting to teach her father to regain his lost literacy. She began each session with flashcards of letters. Both of them ended each session in tears of frustration. Then one day, she printed her name on a card, and her father read it aloud. Meaning had been made.

Most parents keep photo albums of their children, but partly as a parent and partly as a teacher, I have kept a reading journal. Journal writing is becoming more popular as a mode of memoir, and parents and teachers who have discovered this art form know that it can act as a mirror and as a window, reflecting what has happened and opening new worlds of understanding. A journal consists of impressions rather than of factual reports—readers will interpret my words in light of their own lives.

I know that Jay required adults on his journey to literacy, not always as guides or taskmasters, but more often as companions who knew the path and who could help maintain his spirit as he began his print walkabout—wise people prepared to hold his hand, whisper in his ear the secret codes, and pass on the anthem that the difficult journey towards becoming a reader and a writer is worthwhile, even life-giving. It may be that how we accompany children into the print world will determine their future as literate beings.

I have included bits and pieces from my journal to punctuate the ideas under discussion. So much magic is involved in this whole process, and for each boy who makes it into the print circle, we must revel and shout and cry to everyone in sight: *He has learned to read. Alongside us. He joins the circle.*

Literacy Flashbacks
by Jay Booth

I don't remember learning to read. (I know that Sesame Street *was a big influence.) It is as if I always knew how. I do remember being upset with my father when he discarded my Disney books when I was about eight. Mickey holds a special place in my heart, no doubt connected to our Disney World holidays. Although I started reading much earlier, the first thing I can recall reading would be the giant map we had at Phoenix School. Our teacher would place the map on the floor and we would gather around and try to find locations that he called out.*

I have always been a capricious person; I like to do things quickly and move on to the next event. This might explain why record books, sports books, and magazines often piled up on my bed every evening. I enjoyed reading through certain articles or sections, and then moving on to the next selection. The reason Archie comics were so appealing is largely based on their formats. I could read a few strips and move onto something else. They also allowed me to skip around and read whichever strip I wanted, without missing the plot from an earlier one.

I really loved the plays I did during school years. In Phoenix, I was of an age that enjoyed attention (there was never enough), and in the plays, I often got the main part. I was a very hyperactive child (as many boys are), and I loved the physical nature of acting and working on stage. To do this, though, I had to read and memorize the complete scripts, and yet I enjoyed reading all of them, and trying to come up with my own lines to add to them. In Horizon Junior High, I didn't seek attention any longer, but I enjoyed participating in the plays once more, because they were so well-written, and by us students! I loved being in the play that Esther, one of my classmates, wrote and directed. It was such an interesting story of her family's emigration.

I don't remember too many novels from school, the main reason being that we were made to read certain books and often they weren't interesting to me. I do, however, remember reading several by Gary Paulsen and Jerry Spinelli at Horizon. Our teacher, Nancy, often allowed us to select our own novels, and in high school I don't think that was ever an option, something that I think needs to be considered.

As a child I liked to write a lot. I enjoyed trying to come up with novel ideas (mostly trying to make another Lord of the Rings *type novel), and writing letters. I rarely finished anything, and I never had anyone else read what I had* written. It was just quite fun to write all on my own. I believe it helped my imagination to grow, and it also, of course, allowed me to practise my reading and writing.

I don't really remember what my friends read. I do know that my girlfriend loves to escape from university required reading lists with Stephen King, but she doesn't like horror movies. I think that's the thing about reading, as opposed to films: it opens up your imagination and often lets you make your own worlds.

I remember my teacher, Michael, from Phoenix really well. He read to us, and often acted out parts as he was reading. I do remember him also reading on his own when he had time to himself. Nancy, from Horizon, loved to read to her students. I mostly remember her reading poetry.

I know that the computer was, and still is, one of the biggest factors in my development as a reader and writer. Much of my reading nowadays is done on the computer. Visiting message boards and my favorite Web sites are a daily activity. I am also a video game addict, and in spite of what many people may think, some of those games require a great deal of reading. The computer has been a great way for me to engage in literacy activities.

Whenever I get a new CD the first thing I do is look at the liner notes. I like to read the lyrics over once, and for some reason I enjoy reading the acknowledgements.

When it comes to magazines, I read mainly guitar and music varieties. They let me keep up with my favorite bands, and offer choices I can select from. When I read magazines, I actually read them backwards, skimming through, and then I come back to the articles that look interesting.

I do love to read, just not often in novel form. I am working my way through the Harry Potter series at the moment. In contrast to my college reading, my home-time reading is mostly based on the computer, magazines, and sports sections.

A. Understanding the Literacy Lives of Boys

1. Reading is what girls do.

Understanding boys as readers and writers

Travelling Together

If we are separated I will
Try to wait for you on your side of things

Your side of the wall and the water
And of the light moving at its own speed
Even on leaves that we have seen
I will wait on one side

While a side is there

W. S. Marwin

A young teacher came into my office and slumped in the chair on the last day of June. He said, "I taught Grade 8 this year—26 boys and four girls." Right away I knew why he was exhausted. What is the difficulty so many of us find in coping with boys in school? How do we want them to behave? What should boys be like as readers and writers? What is normal literacy behavior?

We don't want to generate or fuel new problems for education and girls as we explore and even promote programs for boys. And there are diverse opinions about the origin and even the nature of the problems that we find inside such a discussion. Most important, the education of boys is closely connected to the education of girls, and school and education policies on gender will directly influence both. If we focus on the problems of boys, do we endanger the efforts of so many in the struggle to bring equity for girls into our society? Or do we see these initiatives as dialogues that are attempting to move us all forward into strengthening the lives of every child as an individual? What if we refuse to consider the issues not as a "war," but as an inquiring into the dynamics of how boys and girls construct their gendered literacy lives?

How can we who work in schools respond fairly to the needs of boys in relation to the needs of girls, and to the diversity among groups of boys and girls? Fortunately, we can benefit from the educational reforms that grew from the changes associated with girls: we can apply those principles of gender equity to the educational needs of boys, even though in many ways, that very system of schooling formerly marginalized girls and privileged some boys. What conditions, then, contain or exacerbate these problems for so many boys and for many girls?

We know that no single category includes all boys or all girls. We don't need to add to the stereotype of classifying all boys' behaviors, tastes and attitudes into one single frame, nor do we want to reinforce the generalities that are often applied to boys. But as we look at studies and reports that examine boys and girls and their learning styles and special interests, their growth patterns and their stages of intellectual development, we do notice differences. These differences are not in all boys or in all girls, but in enough of them to cause us to reflect about our demands on their young lives.

There are definite problems with the ways in which many boys view themselves as literate beings, with how they approach the acts of reading and writing, and with how they respond to assessments of their skills. At least the faltering test scores have opened up discussion on these issues that concern many teachers and parents.

How closely are we watching and interpreting the alarmist data? Are *all* boys at risk? If not, which ones? How significant are developmental stages in boys' literacy abilities? Are there differences in boys' growth with boys of the same age? What is normal literacy achievement for a six-year-old boy? Is it the same for a six-year-old girl? Which boy and which girl? Are we concerned about the girls who are doing poorly? And most important, what do we mean by "literacy"?

Whether the males in our society have been betrayed as Susan Faludi writes, lost or abandoned as William Pollack writes, or treated as losers as Christian Hoff Sommers writes, we are faced with helping them to become proficient readers and writers. To accomplish this complex task, we may need to focus on how gender affects the ways in which boys view themselves as readers and writers.

At the end of every talk I give, parents and teachers line up to ask me questions, and they are almost always about boys in literacy trouble: they don't read, can't read, won't read, don't write, can't write, can't spell. Those of us who are responsible for educating boys are deeply concerned over the plight of many of them who can't or won't enter the literacy club. But our rules for entry are very strict, and oddly enough, computer skills are seldom part of the qualification.

One report from England says that, on average, the higher the parents' income and education, the higher the literacy performance of their children. Socio-economic factors appear to have as much impact on boys' literacy achievements as gender issues. Yet, I can think of dozens of examples where boys have every literacy support conceivable and still don't or can't read, spell or write. Statistics, though, show that most boys in literacy difficulties are from economically troubled families. Among the six million prisoners in the United States, three-quarters of the males are functionally illiterate.

Quality teaching can, of course, overcome the difficulties that children from a lower socio-economic background face when confronting literacy expectations; however, too often schools discriminate (even unconsciously) against some children. The media reports too often describe boys as an under-achieving, educationally disadvantaged group, suffering from the recent support given to girls. Educator Peter Hill suggests we would be better off if we approached the problems by "targeting poorer students, low achievers, picking up disproportionately more boys in the process."

The boys' literacy debate is lined with emotional minefields and requires careful negotiation. Even the terms reveal multiple

"Tomorrow's children will know that all of us, no matter what our color or culture, come from a common mother, way back in Africa millions of years ago. They will appreciate diversity—beginning with the differences between the female and male halves of humanity. They will have mental maps that do not lead to the scapegoating and persecution of those who are not quite like them."

From Tomorrow's Children: A Blueprint for Partnership Education in the 21st Century, *by Riane Eisler*

His night table is carelessly covered
with books that he had shown to a
friend the previous evening—everything from the Story of Ants to
Nobody's Dog (which has been dedi-
cated to him).

Above his bed is a framed and auto-
graphed poster by the author/illustra-
tor Steve Kellogg.

Two tall bookshelves are crammed
with books, neatly arranged by his sit-
ter.

On the corner of his desk sit two
postcards he created earlier that day at
the Ontario Science Centre.

In my pocket is a note to me explaining his absence on my arriving home:

  -I am at Sheleias house. I wil be
  back at 6.

  Jay

    D. B.

Who'd Want to Be a Man

With his heart
a black sack
In which a small
animal's trapped.

With his grief
like a knot
that's tied at birth
balled up and hard.

With his rage
that would smash
the ten thousand things
without blinking.

With his mind
like a tree on a cliff—
its roots, fists
clutching stone

With his longing
that's a dry well
and where is the rain?

  Gregory Orr

definitions: *boys*, *literacy*, *gender*, and *masculinity*. We need to articulate the arguments clearly.

THE WALKABOUT CALLED BOYHOOD

What it means to be a boy or a girl in school is to a large degree dependent upon the school's culture or the classroom's subculture.
How the students define the role of masculinity can be affected by
literacy classrooms and literacy experiences. If schools encourage a
narrow understanding of what masculine behavior should resem-
ble, then that will have an impact on how boys see themselves and
how they are seen by others of both sexes. So much of what boys
read, of how they respond in public, of how they capture their
thoughts and feelings in writing, is determined by the unwritten,
but real expectations of school life.

We need to explore possibilities for promoting change that celebrates and constructs alternative forms of being male in our schools
and in our lives. Countering the popular media's images of the
world of young males is not the only goal of schooling, of course;
however, opening up discussion and offering images of what it
means to be male in certain places at certain times can be a focus
and a concern for every classroom.

Some contemporary educational critics want schools to lead a
movement to alter the dominant versions of masculinity in our society. They want to open up different and multiple forms of behaviors
for boys to consider in our world. They feel that schools are still run
from a fundamentally patriarchal perspective and that the structure
and practice—the mindset of education—has not changed enough
to accommodate any transformation of gender issues for boys or for
girls. Do schools covertly support the traditional roles for boys in the
way they organize and implement programs? The social and cultural concerns about who boys are and who they should become are
tied closely to how schools function, and how schools could approach literacy issues.

There are many recorded instances of teachers requiring and re-
warding different kinds of behavior from girls and from boys, and, of
course, from different individual boys. Altering classroom gender
norms can create risks for both teachers and students, and many
boys have problems accepting their male roles as participants in literacy events. Too often, their own assumptions about masculinity
are challenged. Teachers are faced with finding directions from traditional models of literacy teaching (resources, strategies and student responses) and moving towards a new dynamic of involving
boys in constructing their literacy lives.

As educators, we do want equity in our classrooms; resources that
are bias-free; inclusive or gender-neutral language; and disciplines
that welcome the strengths of different individuals. Men and
women have experienced the world in different ways for a long
time, and the boys and girls we meet in our classrooms come with
different life experiences, knowledge and sets of skills. They are

also at different developmental stages. We do note, with different groups, patterns common to many boys' and girls' behaviors, and the students themselves profess clear definitions of what a boy or a girl is at very early ages. As well, many girls and boys have grown to prefer different subject areas and different learning strategies. In literacy teaching, these factors may cause us to re-evaluate our programs so that boys will view language arts activities as useful or worthwhile, and begin to connect with print-focused learning. Even though many English programs centre on masculine texts that reinforce traditional gender patterns, many boys become alienated from material in these resources. They see literacy endeavors as "feminized," valuing female knowledge and behaviors over their interests.

The norms of gender change constantly. I was extremely surprised one winter to see my son's entire hockey team dye their hair blond. Although this may seem a trivial indication of change, for some boys that I taught in the sixties, having a different hairstyle like the Beatles forced them to leave their homes.

But markers of gender often reveal deeper indications of how boys and girls are defined. Unlike sex, gender is socially constructed, and how it is experienced depends greatly on an individual's social network. What it means to be a boy is continually negotiated, often resisted and sometimes transformed.

Children begin decoding gender long before they decode print. They develop their concepts of gender right from birth, depending on whether they are girls or boys, and gender is certainly a key issue by three or four years of age. How do individuals acquire gender? There are many theories, but none seems to help us fully understand this complex defining process. Very young children, though, notice and respond to visible differences in boys and girls, and some recognize that these gender differences are fundamental to their lives and to how they will interact in society. Nature and nurture have become catch words, but how the brain thinks, how the unconscious works, how the affective and emotional factors relate, how the child is raised, how the social structures surround the child—all of these factors contribute to the child's perception of gender.

Susan Gilbert's *A Field Guide to Boys and Girls* is a helpful advice book for teachers and for parents who want to work with their child's school to build a gender-equitable environment. Gilbert discusses what she feels are natural differences between boys and girls, and offers suggestions for helping schools to avoid sex stereotyping that can affect children's development. She points out that with language operations, male and female brains operate differently. Females use both hemispheres of the brain at once, while males use just the left hemisphere. Stroke victims who are women have an easier time regaining speech than men with similar damage do.

My colleague Kathy Broad has been studying current research in the area of gender differences and the brain. Although far more cognitive similarities than differences exist, there appear to be observable anatomical and chemical differences in the brains of boys and

In Language, Literacy & Gender, *Hillary Minns takes a practical and accessible perspective on gender equity in the literacy classroom. She examines how children naturally fall into gender roles through play and a steady immersion into media, culture, and communication. In her view, "children actively take part in their own socialization into masculine and feminine roles through their language, their dress, the choices they make in games, toys, media heroes, the stories they tell about themselves, and their expectations for the future" (1991, 12).*

girls. For example, girls have an additional language-processing centre in the right frontal lobe, which seems to enhance their capacity to process language. Boys demonstrate greater strength and brain activity in the right hemisphere when utilizing their visual-spatial abilities.

RECOGNIZING SIMILARITIES AND DIFFERENCES BETWEEN BOYS AND GIRLS

We should not alter our expectations for the development of literacy for either gender, but such differences raise a question: What are the best ways and times to present materials and tasks to engage boys and girls in literacy learning? We will need to develop literacy programs that balance different elements and include many strategies that appeal to a variety of learners.

Healthy literacy programs in effective schools create conditions that may help boys to assume different versions of masculinity. Boys need to develop literacy behaviors and skills, but they also need to understand the relationship between gender and how they will read, write and respond.

I am concerned with the fate of many boys now in our schools. We will need to begin where boys are at as they sit in front of us in Language Arts, English, or in any curriculum subject. I want to let the boys I teach know they are valued. Boys will change when they are helped to understand themselves better, are affirmed and valued as they are.

To make meaning of text requires the reader to consider the widest frame around the text and the reading of it. To help boys become literate, we will need to explore what it means to be literate in the "new" times, enhancing literacy success for all students. We will need

- to recognize the differences between some girls and some boys;
- to recognize the similarities between some girls and some boys;
- to identify the diversity within groups of girls and boys;
- to highlight multiple forms of literacy and literate practice;
- to celebrate multiple figurations of masculinity and femininity. (*Boys, Gender and Literacy*)

See how the individual interests of boys and girls are represented successfully in the text that follows. As a picture book, it was a collaborative venture among boys and girls in second grade. It represents for me the achievement of their common goal of constructing and telling a story through words and pictures.

"The term Pack Rules *has a dual meaning. As a noun it is a list of mandates about how boys should act. As a verb, when the "pack rules," it describes how boys' inner lives become dominated by these mandates. Both usages are apt descriptions of how boys often learn to become men in mainstream American culture."*

From Boy Talk, *by Mary Polce-Lynch*

Snow White in Toronto

Once upon a time there was a girl named Snow White. she lived in the Royal York Hotel in Toronto with her mother.

The seven hockey players on her team put their jerseys down on the floor and lay Snow White down on them.

Page 6

Snow White in Toronto

Written and illustrated
by Brian Leah Riannon John
Manny Emily Alyssa

Once upon a time there was a girl named Snow White. She lived in the Royal York Hotel in Toronto with her mother.

Her favourite sport was hockey and she played on Toronto Maple Leafs at Maple Leaf Gardens.

One day her mother married a man who wanted to be the best hockey player in the world. When he saw Snow White playing hockey on TV he was very jealous. After the game was over, he went up to her and said, "I want to challenge you to a hockey game. I'll have Bester and you'll have Ron Hextall."

In the first period Snow White scored three goals. In the second period the stepfather scored three goals.

At intermission the stepfather put poison in her water bottle. When she drank the water, she fell down and it looked like she was dead.

The seven hockey players on her team put their jerseys down on the floor and lay Snow White down upon them.

One of the players, Gretsky, was a doctor, and he gave her respiration, and she spit out the water and sat up.

They went back on the ice for the third period and Snow White got the winning goal.

The referee sent the stepfather to the penalty box for seven hundred years.

Snow White fell in love with Gretsky, and a week later they got married and played hockey on the same team happily ever after.

Nobody makes sense like girls do. My girlfriends and I can verbally hammer out a dilemma, discuss every facet and angle until the world makes sense and everyone else can sod off. Until telepathy reigns, the only way to reach an understanding is to talk about that inside stuff. Boys can't do that. What is so hard about emotional analysis that boys can't do it? . . .

If someone had scientific proof that communication through discussion was not the right way to get to a greater truth, sure I'd explore options. If there was some relationship rain dance, there are times during arguments that I would gladly throw up my arms, get outside and jump around to make things better.

I guess people really should come with manuals, but then I've never read a manual anyway. We should probably talk about this.

Hannah Sung, in The Toronto Star, *Tuesday, August 20, 2002*

Our propensity in education to "measure" school success through high-stakes testing continues to magnify gender differences. To be sure, researchers need to continue to examine the relationship between girls' and boys' test scores and grades, but they must also complexify this work by attending responsibly to the relationships between school success and achievement broken down by many categories of identity and social positioning such as: sex, race, ethnicity, disability, and class. This kind of data will help to develop appropriate equity responses and interventions based on individual differences. Commonly, researchers report that girls suffer silent losses in classrooms, while boys' problems are loud enough to be heard throughout the school. It is my view, however, that these stories of "success" and "failure" are a great deal more complex.

My own research in a diverse Toronto public secondary school for girls would suggest that assumptions about gender, race, class and ethnicity need to be brought into view—without calcifying these "differences"—in order to allow girls and boys to both recognize constructs of power at play in social relations and imagine other ways of relating to and learning from those different from ourselves.

Kathleen Gallagher

As a student in a girls' private school, gender bias was really not an issue in my own early education. We were expected to develop literacy skills as well as math and science skills . . . The only students who could be good at math and science were girls and the only students who could be good at reading were also girls. It seems like such a simple conclusion, but it wasn't a topic I had ever considered. I never thought about the fact that I did not have to compete with males in the classroom. As a result, by the time I arrived in Grade 9 in a co-ed school, I think I had developed enough confidence as a student that it was not as much of an issue. I am sure this is a significant reason why gender roles and biases have not been a significant topic of consideration for me as a teacher.

Speaking with friends about gender biases, many of my male friends report being endlessly bored with the language curriculum in elementary school. Many could not even name a single book that they had read in school. Most of them admitted to never reading for pleasure and said that the only type of reading they found satisfying or pleasurable was reading for information. This reinforced for me that my educational experience in a single gender school was a unique one and that gender bias in all areas of instruction is a significant concern.

Sarah Kochhar

---

2. My father only reads the newspaper.

Providing literacy models for boys

How does a boy learn to be male, and to be a reader and writer? If boys are disadvantaged by the texts that teachers choose, by some of the topics in the curriculum, or by resources that poorly match their needs and interests, do we perpetuate stereotypes if we redress these concerns? Or, do we begin where boys are and offer alternatives? In English classes, adolescent males must handle a curriculum where the focus is on narrative genre, and emotional and creative responses. Because traditional male roles downplay the expressing and sharing of feelings, emotions, and experiences of others, boys may be unwilling to discuss some kinds of texts. And in many school cultures, achieving and demonstrating a commitment to academic goals are seen as "unboy" and unmasculine behavior. Sue Pidgeon, in *Boys and Reading*, says that "The drive for equality of opportunity in the 1970's has resulted in a much wider range of options and behaviors for girls but does not seem to have been matched with a similar expansion for boys."

But changing times do not favor anyone whose reading and writing skills are lacking. Males who leave school early or who have poor literacy skills used to have an edge in the labor market because employers favored them for heavy manual jobs. However, jobs requiring muscle are disappearing and are unlikely to return. New jobs require an ability to communicate well, and communication includes reading and writing as well as speaking.

Today, many more fathers are showing interest in the literacy lives of their children. But I notice in my classes and in my talks to teachers that very few men attend sessions on children's literature, or on reading and writing. A few more sign up each year, but literacy education is still a field dominated by women. This factor is not necessarily negative in the lives of boys, but I do worry about boys being able to observe males within the literacy cultures—men who read and write in a variety of genres, interacting with each other and building cooperatively a deeper understanding of the issues they are reading about.

Consider these questions. Have boys ever seen their fathers (or any males connected to the family) reading? If so, what texts were being read? What influences in the reading lives of their children do mothers have? Do boys see men reading at school? What, if any, influence does a lack of male literacy models have on a boy? And, of course, how is his literacy environment conditioned further by the media he watches and listens to?

Boys learn to be literate, just as girls do. Being male and being a reader are closely linked, especially in our present society. How will a boy develop a reading identity that allows him membership in the literacy club and in his friendship circle at the same time? How is a "reading boy" or a "non-reading boy" constructed?

In *Stiffed*, Susan Faludi journeys "through a post war male realm." She reports on the complicated issues involved in being boys and men in today's society, and on the changes in what it now means and feels like to be male. She presents how men see themselves as brothers, fathers, lovers, husbands, uncles, and workers. Through interviews, observations and analysis, Faludi tells the compelling stories of dozens of men, incarnations of malehood as it has evolved over the last 50 years. As you read, you cannot help but be amazed and moved by the cultural forces that construct and confuse men as they struggle with the politics of gender roles. She says that "the problem of what boys were doing to the world was rooted in what the world was doing to boys."

What does school do to boys and to girls? What stories will the boys and girls tell about reading and writing during their school years?

Research finds four factors that contribute to men who are fathers rejecting reading as a voluntary activity:

- Reading and physical activity are defined as mutually exclusive.
- Fictional narrative is rejected.
- Reading is seen as a forced activity, like homework.
- Interest in maths and science is viewed as opposition to literature.

We need to model literacy as parents and teachers, especially with male role models. We can do this by sharing materials and experiences from our own lives as readers and writers. We can also

A young male student teacher, on the last day of his course, shouted out: "I never have to read a book again!" Of course, he was responding to the routine of essay writing from required texts and articles after five years at university, but I wonder what he will choose to read during his career as a teacher and, in his life, as a man.

D. B.

demonstrate techniques and strategies for boys so that they can continue to grow as literate beings.

Here are some initiatives in modeling literacy.

- In Great Britain, a group of fathers and elder brothers were involved in sharing material from book bags designed for struggling boy readers. Targeted at boys of eight and nine, kits on more than 30 different topics were put into sports bags. Each bag included a non-fiction book, related activities and a magazine for adults. Several schools have now adopted the project for their own purposes.

- Jan Greer, in her study, describes one boy who showed significant improvement in his reading abilities once his dad and granddad became aware of his low ability. The boy's dad and granddad began providing a supportive environment by reading with him, supplying him with age-appropriate, interesting reading materials and helping him with his reading. The attention and interest shown by his family boosted the boy's confidence and performance.

- Heather Richmond and Cheryl Miles are investigating the effects of a Male Mentor Reading Program on boys. The project assumed that male athletes would provide young boys and girls with an ideal male (who liked to read). This assumption was based on notions of the lack of male elementary teachers, the consequently feminized school and the need for father figures for under-fathered boys. Richmond and Miles hope to invite a broader range of university-educated men to join them, to establish a read-aloud book collection, for example. They are closely considering just what masculinities these mentors are constructing as they read to the children. The varsity hockey players, by virtue of their star status, are symbols of a form of masculinity.

Dad loved reading. When I was no longer a difficult young woman and Dad needed more than his mates, we started to talk about books. Once, I remember, he had just finished reading A. B. Facey's A Fortunate Life. *A wonderful book, he said. As good as* The Old Man and the Sea. *"You can tell," he said, "that Hemingway's the writer, but Facey's got a better story to tell." At the time, precious though this conversation was to me, it didn't strike me as remarkable. Now, I wonder if it doesn't mark the passing of an age: when a man could die and leave his daughter—though it could just as*

easily be his son—not only his football trophies, but the books and writers that mattered to him.

Addy Wright

Reading was something that was just done in my family. We were never told to read, or lectured to about the value of reading or the appropriateness of certain books. However my parents would allow me to stay up as late as I wanted to, if I was reading; be it comic book, textbook, or novel. My brothers and I shared a bedroom. They wouldn't let me leave the light on to read, but my bed was pushed next to the window. Light from a

street lamp streamed over my bed and I can remember reading adventure stories late into the night, listening to the footsteps of the people coming and going from the house across the street, imagining they were characters from the stories I read.

The librarian in my elementary school had an interesting way of encouraging reading. She had a storage room in the school library. If you finished the assigned reading quickly you were allowed to go into the musty storage room and select one of the many old hard-cover books, which lined the shelves. She told us the school

19

board had banned these books because they were either too difficult or inappropriate for our young minds. I used to love going into that room to select a book. The librarian made you feel that only special people were allowed into that room. It was in that storage room where I was first introduced to Edgar Rice Burroughs, Jules Verne and Charles Dickens. Tarzan, Phileas Fogg and Sydney Carton were real people to me. I wished I could transport myself to Mars in the wink of an eye like John Carter or join Professor Lidenbrock as he journeyed to the centre of the earth.

Ron Lynd

I see myself as a reader—I read newspapers, magazines, anything interesting.

At work I review reports, but that type of reading is different because I have to do it for my job. There is no real sense of enjoyment. It's not like reading a magazine where, if I don't want to read the article then I just turn the page. At work, I just can't skip a report or else I'm fired. It's like having to read all of those books in high school—Othello, To Kill a Mockingbird, Death of a Salesman, etc. . . .

In order to read, you must have some time. When I have some free time, it is seldom spent reading. There is just so much more to do. Reading is low on the list of priorities. Reading was never fun for me. I was always told what I had to read and that turned me off of reading. I think we spent too much time analyzing things and writing book reports and that took the fun out of print.

Office worker

3. I would rather watch television.

Constructing a reader

If reading is about the interaction between reader and text, if making sense of print demands background that can shape our interpretations and understanding of the author's intent and words, why would gender not be considered a significant factor? We bring everything we are to a text, struggling to fit what we read into our world picture. We make sense of print text with the texts of our lives. We bring our past and our present to our reading. Being a boy is part of how our male students read, and for some boys, it is a dominant force.

If some boys see reading as a feminized activity (especially if we define literacy as reading novels), then they will reject it. Usually, peer groups demand gender-specific behavior. For those boys who want to belong, it will be difficult to reveal themselves as readers who read what "outside members" read. More important, it will be hard to respond emotionally or sensitively to what has been read, while others of their group are present. Also, if the boys are limited readers, they face the chance of failure or of seeming incompetent in these literacy activities. Thus, the avoidance, reluctance and resistance of so many boys to enter the "literature circle."

Which of us reinforces the socially constructed notions of how boys should interact with particular books? I have observed and talked to dozens of men—educated teachers, many in graduate programs—who have made definite decisions not to engage in emotional and reflective reading activities. As one said to me: "Joining a book club? I'm afraid that's not for me." But I also know of a male teacher in New York who meets his friend at the bar every

Wednesday at 4:30 p.m. to have a beer and talk about the book they have agreed to read. The teacher values this time, as does his friend, and they negotiate book choice carefully. They each benefit from the dialogue. But there are few book clubs for men. What should we do with boys?

Let us consider how we can positively affect not just our students' abilities in literacy, but their attitudes towards living as readers and writers throughout their lives. See "Bringing Boys into Literacy" on pages 111–112 for questions about reading and gender.

BOYS, GIRLS AND READING

In one study, the researcher found that while both boys and girls had read the same adventure novels, they had taken different things from them. The girls responded to the feelings of the characters, how their personalities had been shaped by their pasts; the boys enjoyed the action and found that the reflective portions detracted from the story. Having spent almost every Friday night with my son at the movies, I know that his choices always involved action "teen" flicks with superheroes and action men. What is normal?

When I ask groups of male and female teachers to tell me the books they read as children, the women call them out quickly: "Nancy Drew," "Trixie Belden," "Judy Blume," and yes, "The Hardy Boys." The men sometimes hitchhike on the women's titles. The women all say they read "The Hardy Boys," but I have yet to meet a man who, as a boy, read *Anne of Green Gables*. Girls read "boy" books, but they read them differently. For boys, reading a book assigned to girls presents much larger problems, often based on gender images of self as seen by others.

Some boys and girls read and enjoy the same novels. In classrooms that create a literacy subculture, boys are freed from many of the social expectations that deny them access. They can respond to more reflective selections.

My colleague, Shelley Peterson, is exploring gender influences on adolescents' writing choices and on teachers' assessment of student writing. Her research shows that most teachers perceive girls to be better writers than boys. Also, many students perceive girls to be better writers than boys. The perception that writing reveals information about the sexual identities of the writers limits student choices of topics, characters and genres. Adolescent boys, in particular, write with an awareness that writing in ways that are typically associated with girls would result in negative social consequences.

Out-of-school literacy practices for many boys often go unrecognized or untapped in the school classroom. What boys value as literacy texts can unintentionally be dismissed or demeaned in school. And yet for many boys, their deep involvement in (and their dedication to) computers, magazines, CD-ROMs, videos, card collections and hobbies can offer us entry points into their lives as readers and writers.

From the adventures contained in early serials (ancestors of our modern-day comic books) to the mysteries solved by the Hardy Boys, series fiction has always held a strong appeal for boys. Rowling's Harry Potter books offer both the familiarity of a recurring cast of characters and thrilling mysteries that must be solved in each book.

Literacy Behaviors in Boys and Girls

These research snippets are drawn from the writings listed in Professional Reading.

- Boys often speak their first words later than girls and develop clear speech about a year and a half later.
- Girls have more practice with words right from the beginning. Parents talk more to their daughters than to their sons. Girls' friendships seem to continue that practice, as they share intimacies and decode emotional responses.
- Boy's fine motor skills lag behind those of girls by about a year. As toddlers, boys may show greater interest in exploring the environment.
- In Clark's study of self-taught readers, the boys made use of environmental print, while the girls enjoyed repeated readings of familiar patterned books.
- In a 30-word spelling test for seven-year-olds, boys, on average, misspelled six more words than girls.
- Boys are two to five times more likely than girls to have a reading disability. They also have greater difficulty overcoming it.
- Boys are more prone to some speech and language difficulties. Four times as many boys as girls stutter.
- Boys are more likely than girls to be placed in remedial reading classes or to be held back a grade.
- Girls do better on standardized tests of reading comprehension, writing, spelling and grammar. They speak more fluently, think of words they want to say more quickly, and make fewer grammar and pronunciation errors.
- Boys rank lower in their class and earn fewer honors than girls.
- In South Australia, Malcolm Slade found that boys thought school was boring with too many bad teachers; they thought girls were treated better than boys and that adults seldom listened to what boys had to say.
- Women read more than men. They read more books, and they read more fiction. Julia Hodgeon says young girls get more reading practice because they seek it, often staying close to their mothers and female teachers and benefiting from literacy-related activities.
- Boys have much less interest in leisure reading. They read more for utilitarian purposes than girls do.
- Boys' reading experiences at home were likely to be adult-initiated.
- More boys than girls label themselves "non-readers" (nearly 50 percent by high school).
- Boys appear to be more enthusiastic about reading electronics texts than girls.
- Poetry is less popular with boys than girls.
- Girls are far readier to read books about boys than boys are to read books about girls.
- Some boys are passionate about reading fantasy and science fiction.
- Boys prefer active responses to reading instead of talking about the text with others.
- Boys require more teacher attention in co-ed classrooms.
- Boys are over-represented in special classes for emotional and behavioral disturbances.
- Girls are better at grasping the nuances of feelings and relationships in fictional texts. They also write more affectively.
- Boys who choose non-traditional subjects or activities not seen as masculine enough are teased, bullied and harassed; they thereby learn to avoid opportunities for literacy and literacy growth.
- Many boys are discouraged from responding emotionally to fictional texts by their families and by experiences with peer groups. Lower comprehension scores may be the result.
- Girls are far freer to act out male roles than boys are to act out female roles.

Boys and girls enter school with different sets of strengths and challenges. As Susan Gilbert says, though, "Biological differences may endow boys and girls with different strengths and weaknesses to start with, but experience shows they don't close doors. Boys and girls achieve the same overall scores on several different intelligence tests. It is estimated that a child's general IQ is 30 percent to 40 percent inherited genetics. The remainder is shaped by the quality of life experiences."

Jack was considered "at risk" for literacy development due to his home environment. Both of Jack's parents are from Portugal and work as cleaners. They are both anxious for him to succeed at school so that he will not become a cleaner. Any assigned homework is always completed and returned on time. His father becomes critical when he doesn't do well and views him in terms of "a loser." Consequently, Jack has a tremendous fear for failure. He is not allowed to bring home library books because of the risk of overdue fines. His father speaks English; however, his mother's English is minimal. They are illiterate in English and therefore possibly unable to provide role models for reading and writing. Accordingly, his teacher compensates for this by providing a role model.

Jack's fear of failure has been diminished by the consistent and positive approach of his teacher. His English fluency has increased as a result of the warm and accepting climate in the classroom. This has enabled Jack to contribute more ideas in class discussions and he is ready to benefit from feedback. Jack is asking more questions and showing even more involvement in stories. He is able to predict and anticipate outcomes.

Student teacher

As a youngster, I would think to myself, why should I read when there are so many more fun and exciting things to do? I could hang out with my friends, play hockey, even go to work at my father's restaurant. Anything to avoid reading and writing. I would sometimes think, who in the world reads and writes for fun? Why would anyone want to keep a diary? Why read when you can watch the movie? The only thing worth reading is the Sports section of the paper! I can go on, but the point is rather clear.

In school, I don't recall reading being much fun. I remember a lot of stories followed by question and answer periods. There was a great deal of time spent on penmanship (my handwriting is still atrocious). One cannot forget the book report. All you had to do was look at the summary (usually on the back cover) and rephrase it. There was no way the teacher could pin you down on that. Finally, there was the much dreaded journal. I don't know what it was with some of my teachers. Why in the world did we have to keep those things?

Teacher

In Grade 1, my nephew David was one of the students who the teacher considered as being a "late bloomer." Apparently, he did not read at school like many of the other children. In school he was usually engaged in any activity other than reading. As his aunt, I knew that David enjoyed listening to bedtime stories. I would often read to him his favourite books. One was Green Eggs and Ham *and the other was* How the Grinch Stole Christmas. *He also enjoyed* Sleeping Dragons *by Sheree Fitch. He loved rhyming books and books that made him laugh. Most of all I knew he was happy. I remember telling his mother not to worry. David would start to read on his own when he was ready. David did start to read in his own time and now in Grade 4 he is a fluent reader.*

It is true that some children gravitate to reading early . . . Such children seem to learn to read on their own . . . But such children are in the minority. Studies by my colleagues and myself, and by other investigators, find that only one to three children in 100 read proficiently (at the second grade level) on entrance to Kindergarten. If learning to read was as easy as learning to talk, as some writers claim, many more children would learn to read on their own. The fact that they do not, despite being surrounded by print, suggests that learning to read is not a spontaneous or simple skill . . . The majority of children can, however, learn to read with ease if they are not hurried into it.

Primary teacher

4. We never get to choose the books in school.

Giving boys choice and ownership in their reading

In listening to and reading the dozens of interviews we carried out for this book, it became evident that too many male respondents view themselves as non-readers. However, in almost all cases, they were referring to the reading of literature, specifically fictional novels. Most respondents actually read a great deal, but seldom novels, and most expressed guilt (or even shame) about this. Interestingly, I also find myself reading mainly non-fiction at this time in my life.

When I mentioned this lack of novels in so many men's lives to a woman colleague, she commented, "How sad." But many of these men's lives seem full and satisfying. My barber, as well as two couples I know, travel around the world to attend opera events while I stay at home. Is that a sadness in my life? Or, does it represent one of the many choices that I make from the world of arts events that I select and celebrate?

The novels mentioned by the men in our surveys tended to represent a particular genre—espionage and mysteries—such as the books by Ken Follett, John Grisham, and John Irving. However, there were anomalies—the Harry Potter series, which has attracted many adult male readers because of its fantasy theme, media connection, and significantly, the fact that several were either reading to or alongside their sons, voluntarily sharing in a type of intergenerational, same-sex book club. I shouldn't omit the success of *Lord of the Rings* either: the movie tie-ins have resulted in enormous sales, mainly to males.

What I choose to read depends upon such a variable list of factors. In my teaching, I long ago stopped thinking that there was a master list of what everyone should read. Instead, I moved towards supporting readers' decisions about the print resources they select —their newspapers, their novels, their magazines, their work and organizational materials, and what they read for fun and games. As with films and television, appreciating literature is a developmental, lifelong process, dependent on many factors—personal background, language and thinking skills, life experiences, familiarity with the type of selection, the purpose and payoff for reading, and the situation in which the reading is taking place. It especially depends on the readers' attitudes towards texts, often determined by their school experiences. What I want to do now is open up the options that print resources can offer and explore with boys how different texts work—what to look for and what to expect—so that they can be informed about the choices they will make and select the resources that will give them the most satisfaction. Often, that depends on the quality of the writing, whether it is the daily editorial or the gardening book just purchased that spring.

Good books matter to the literacy lives of young people and I have always sought them out. I have worked with children, teachers and parents for decades attempting to persuade them that a curriculum full of worthwhile books is one of hope for enriching young people's lives.

But I have changed my views on what matters most: I want each reader to determine what he will read and to approach each text confidently, critically, and perhaps appreciatively. For example, sports columnists, such as Roger Angell, can outwrite many, if not most, of the writers commenting on entertainment. Why can't we help interested boys to find those selections, read them carefully, and consider both the implications of the content and the effect of the style?

Rather than write about appreciation of literature, I am choosing to focus on *literacy* as the goal of developing readers and writers. The term *literature* refers to one particular and significant art form that I hope, in some form, will be available to the boys in our schools.

Having said that, I am disheartened when literature specialists such as Harold Bloom want to decide what literature should mean to everyone and spend their lives telling us what we should or should not have read. Certainly for those who want to enjoy this art form and are able to do it, these "must read" lists can guide (and motivate) our choices. But that is not for everyone.

The literary canon for adolescents has not altered much over the last 30 or 40 years. The same novels are used throughout most school districts in North America, without much awareness of equity or gender issues, or whether young people are being prepared for a life with literature. *Catcher in the Rye*, *To Kill a Mockingbird*, *Lord of the Flies*, and *A Separate Peace* appear on virtually every class booklist. They are often read and analyzed chapter by chapter, with too little attention paid to the impact of choice and teaching strategy on the future literacy lives of the students. Many men in our surveys commented again and again on their dislike of these novels, and why they would not choose similar reading materials again.

We need to consider how schools select their novels. Are they bridging the development of the students with literature that they can access and connect to? Are there teaching strategies that would support young readers in handling a sophisticated British novel, with resources that open up the themes and content of the book with the texts (film and print) that they have already experienced? Do we care what boys think about what they are made to read, or is this just one of the bitter pills that, when digested, will make them better citizens? Of course, some adolescent males enjoy these books, and continue to enrich their lives with literature. But too many others are left feeling guilty and inadequate as readers. Often, those boys who learn to read later than girls can't catch up with reading novels and extended forms of narrative fiction. Yet many teachers give priority to this type of literacy activity.

> **From Counting Stars**
> *by David Almond*
>
> *Then he'd ask about books, and we'd start to smile. He knew that the library had begun to overcome the church. The library was a prefabricated place on a green beside the square. I took out armfuls of Hemingway and Lawrence and now forgotten names from the Recommended New Novels section. I pored in excited confusion through The Waste Land and The Cantos. I learned Dylan Thomas and Steve Smith by heart. I plundered the shelves of the paranormal. I devoured surveys of the occult, read tantalizing accounts of spontaneous combustion, the aura teleportation, poltergeists and human vanishings. I took home books on yoga and propped them on the bedroom floor and attempted the Plow or the Lotus or teetered upside down on my head.*

How can we help boys who are reluctant readers to read what educators call literature? The goal is to enable them to interpret and appreciate the literature they will experience throughout their lives, without setting a frame of shame or humiliation. We know that we read the same book through different eyes as we grow into our lives, and often we are shocked at our new response to a text we thought we knew with our hearts and minds. Across time, my accumulated experiences from research, reading, and relationships have altered my responses and reactions. Similarly, students construct their meanings with a particular book from the viewpoint of their own developing experiences. We would not want them to respond to a book at 12 years of age in the same way as a 40-year-old father would. Who they are at a particular stage in life will determine to a great extent how they interact with a particular text.

As teachers, we have all experienced the disappointment that comes from a student revealing his boredom or dissatisfaction with what we had felt was a significant piece of literature. Finding appropriate and interesting books for our students is a complicated task, but it is at the centre of our struggle to help them become appreciative readers intent on extending their own knowing. (If only they would enjoy what we told them to enjoy, or like a book because we did!) Backgrounds and abilities differ widely in the boys we meet, and we need to help them begin to consider their responses to text, to reflect on why they feel as they do, and to consider the author's role in determining how they responded to a particular selection.

For so many of us, how and what we read today is different from even the nearby past. We choose materials that can easily be handled in short bursts of time; we browse and sample newspapers, professional journals, magazines, Web sites—smaller snippets of text—and struggle to find time for longer items such as novels and biographies. Many selections are highly visual, filled with colored illustrations, detailed drawings and photographs, with a variety of fonts and sizes. Just notice how newspapers have changed their formats and styles for a public that reads differently from the past.

Young people are bombarded with so much stimuli from television, cereal boxes, advertising, and computer games. How will a text medium full of long, uninterrupted print passages compete with the visual and aural sensations that beat upon them and catch them in Ron Jobe's "web of immediacy"? Can we use the range of powerful literature that we have access to today for motivating reluctant readers into exploring the ideas, the other worlds, the information, the surprises, the sense of imagination contained inside the very books they too often disdain? What if these readers could find themselves engaged in a powerful book that they couldn't put down? What would change in their reading lives? Would they forget for the moment their reading difficulties and simply read? Why are some teachers and parents able to find the right books for those children at such a difficult stage in their reading lives? A tall order, but for many non-reading boys, a possibility. A significant experience with a suitable book can give boys something to focus on besides their anxiety over being limited readers.

As parents and teachers, we could begin by providing all of our young people with a large quantity, a wide range and a great variety of experiences with the genre of story. We could offer all kinds of narratives, including fiction (fairy tales, folk tales, realistic fiction, novels, legends, mysteries, fantasies, adventures), non-fiction books (diaries, biographies, encyclopedias, atlases, memoirs), poetry anthologies and picture books. Exposure to a wide range of books offers them a chance to be involved in some of the things they are reading, to be emotionally engaged with print experiences—some boys for the first time. As well, limited readers would gain the opportunity to learn how authors use language, since the language of literature differs from the language of daily conversations, often offering a richer vocabulary and more complex sentence structure, imagery, and phrasing.

In her moving picture book *Mr. Lincoln's Way*, Patricia Polacco features a boy in trouble, a rebellious non-reader who is sent to the principal's office because of his racial name-calling. Mr. Lincoln finds time to work with this boy, and like other fine administrators I have met, develops a plan to assist him in learning to read. Hearing about the hobby of the boy's grandfather—bird watching—the principal sets up a site just outside his office so that each day the two of them can observe the geese in a small pond. This approach softens the boy's attitude, and he begins to reveal more about his life and struggles.

I always trust this author to take me deeply inside the lives of others, and to help me recognize the need for self-worth in all of us. In this story, Polacco offers us hope for working with the I-can't/I-won't-read boy: we must search for a place to begin, a starting point for understanding what print holds. Only then will that I-might-read child stumble into what we know already, so that both of us can feel another's thoughts captured in print, for the rest of our lives, whenever we choose. Ann Lamott says it best: "Bird by bird." Word by word.

I learned more about gender observations from reading books by Vivian Gussin Paley than I have from any other resource. She paints such vivid pictures of boys and girls playing and learning in her early years classroom, as the children explore books she has shared with them through dramatic play, painting and conversations. When teachers such as Paley create narrative communities, the joy of learning is obvious. Teachers and parents of older children will benefit greatly from Paley's journeys of discovery. Her books include The Girl with the Brown Crayon, Wally's Stories *and* The Boy Who Would Be a Helicopter *(my favorite one of them all).*

D. B.

How can we go about discovering the real reading interests of boys? They will need to make choices in their literacy lives—to sense ownership of their reading and writing selves—by having opportunities to select some of the books they read, the topics they write about, and the projects they research. They will care more about the activities that they feel are their own and will want to invest their time and interest in them.

Three examples of boys' choices follow.

Sports articles, such as that on Tony Hawk, a 34-year-old skateboard star, appeal to many boys. I clip them and add them to my growing collection of examples of literacy. Often, the weekend papers, which are available to schools on Mondays, hold such resources for boys and literacy.

Michael, who taught boys in Grade 10 who were having great difficulty in literacy, attempted to collect all types of narratives that his students might want to read. He perused the school anthologies, the new and old ones in the bookroom; he went on-line to talk to other teachers about selections that had worked with their students, and he amassed a useful literature collection of short, powerful pieces that could function as starting points in building reading success with his remedial readers. Interestingly, their favorite selection was that hoary old chestnut "The Monkey's Paw"; they wanted more stories like that one.

In my Grade 8 drama classes at a middle school, my most successful lesson revolved around a collection of old British play books that had been left in the room many years earlier. Students worked in twos or threes, selected a one-act play, read it silently, and then prepared it for sharing over the next two weeks. It gave me such delight to see these boys and girls interpreting these old theatre scripts, full of unfamiliar British expressions and archaic vocabulary, about issues far away from their contemporary young lives. The sharing times were full of fun and hard words, with the observers struggling to make sense as their classmates brought these period pieces to life. It shouldn't have been a successful unit, but it was my favorite that year.

We need boys to enter the classroom culture alongside the home culture and the corner-store culture. Keeping all these layers of identity together will allow schools to be the winners. With solid strategies for reflection and critical thought, perhaps we can move the students towards challenging their own and society's assumptions about literacy issues.

Here's an example of home culture supporting classroom culture. At college, my son Jay took an English course where they looked at vocabulary lists once a month. There were strange, unfamiliar words they had to memorize for tests. On the third such test, he phoned to say it was extremely simple and we realized that the words were all from mythologies. He had learned them from the computer games that had co-opted them into their lexicon. Similarly, environmental print becomes significant for boys who are

---

Flying high at 34, skateboard star Tony Hawk is the Martha Stewart of his sport

Like his Raptor namesake, Tony Hawk spends most of his time in the air. Hawk, arguably the world's most accomplished professional skateboarder, is bringing his jaw-dropping skateboard skills to Toronto's SkyDome tomorrow during the Argos game as part of his international tour.

Of course, no show is complete without his signature 900 move, which consists of a 360-degree double somersault. It's one of more than 80 gravity-mocking moves he's invented over his 18-year career.

Krystyna Lagowski, in
The Toronto Star,
Thursday, August 22, 2002

learning to read—signs, memos, labels, and directions all add to their literacy vocabulary base.

Many boys are drawn to reading the same book over and over again. I used to think they needed the sense of success it would bring, but now I feel that they have a desire to experience that story again, like those of us who watch a favorite film or a rerun of *Seinfeld.* One boy I remember read *Charlotte's Web* (and only *Charlotte's Web*) from Grades 2 to 7. When the Grade 7 teacher noticed the level of choice and inquired, the boy said he had loved the book ever since the Grade 2 teacher had read it aloud. Imagine the safety net for that child during all those years of independent reading, always knowing the story and never having to be afraid of being unable to handle an unknown book.

But this conjures up in my mind Michael, a lad in Grade 6 who chose *Treasure Island* as his independent book. He was a boy at risk as a reader, and when I tried to intervene, he told me that his older brother had read it, and there was nothing more he wanted in the world than to be like his brother. And read it he did, painstakingly slowly, for three months. Now, with my experiences in literacy, would I have handled him differently? Probably not. Reading *Treasure Island* was his mission, and he achieved it.

COMICS

I have never quite understood the hostility that many teachers and parents have towards comics for children. Consider the long, international popularity of comics such as Asterix the Gaul and Tintin, selling in the hundreds of millions. Archie comics kept my son occupied through many long plane rides, and when I was 12 my own collection included all of the Marvel comic heroes, especially Batman. (I remember when color was removed from comics, leaving them printed in black and white to deaden their impact on young boys' literacy values—to no avail. Color soon returned.) But generalities are always full of holes. Years ago, during a sleepover with a childhood friend, Robert, he and I trundled off to bed where we were allowed to read for a time. I read my comics; he read an anthology of animal stories by Ernest Thompson Seton. At the time I wondered why Robert would make such a choice; now I include one of Seton's stories in every anthology I write for children.

Today, comics are still preferred reading for boys, especially for those who are labeled reluctant readers. Many educators consider comics as sub-literature, but some teachers have used comics in the classroom and achieved remarkable results. Students are able to visualize and construct meaning because of the blend of pictures and text. To many adults (generally males), comics represent an art form with critical attributes just like any other.

It seems that comic books and magazines became a useful device for acquiring literacy in Japan. It is common to see male students wearing school uniforms and middle-class male workers wearing suits reading comic magazines on urban trains. For those who need to be on a train for an hour, it can be enjoyable to read a comic magazine, ten different stories of more than 400 pages, instead of buying a bigger, flimsy newspaper that can be an obstacle for other people in crowded trains. Girls are not prone to read in public places; they seem to prefer reading at home. These comic magazines are produced weekly and can be bought not only at bookstores but also platform kiosks and 24-hour convenience stores for only 2–3 Canadian dollars. This weekly production cycle promotes the purchase of the next issues.

Masayuki Hachiya

CLASSICS

Many parents want their boys to read the classics of long ago. Today, experienced and able readers still enjoy them, but as reading tastes and writing styles change, readers may make alternative choices. Boys can find in the classics a different life from their own in language, custom, place, time, or circumstance; for some, these differences can make the reading difficult. Reading classics aloud permits adults to interpret the stories. Independent readers may relish the depth of language and content that make up classics, often, the media repopularize an old book and breathe new life into it. On the whole, though, we should tread lightly in pushing these books, recognizing that our goal is literacy for boys within the richest viable context we can create for them.

FICTION AND NON-FICTION

Teachers tell me of the boys in their classes seeking out information books, hoping to find one that speaks of what they know, with minimal text, free of idioms and expressions and subtext, and full of visuals. Many boys, including a large proportion of reluctant or limited readers, opt for non-fiction, reading for a specific purpose, getting information, figuring out what happens, making things, keeping track of things and helping others. (See "Non-Fiction" at the end of Recommended Books for Boys.)

Ron Jobe says that reluctant readers want action, raw humor, familiarity and complex illustrations; in contrast, teachers prefer elegance of story structure, sophistication of character development, complexity of description, irony and references to other literature. Of course, many boys read fictional stories, especially action stories where what the characters do is usually more important than what they think or feel. These are stories of adventure, horror and ghosts, science fiction, sports, war and spies. We see these themes continued in the best sellers most enjoyed by men.

***From* Boys and Books**
by James Moloney

School students who read nothing but fiction may get through a prodigious number of books. They may even win English prizes. But they have narrowed their reading interests and experience to a harmful degree. Political, economic and social empowerment comes to those who use their skills to engage the full range of reading material available —from information books, biographies and newspapers to magazines and comics.

The aim, then, for both boys and girls, is a healthy balance. In this way, young people—whatever their sex—can become both "people literate" and empowered in the wider world. Fiction has much to offer within this balance, but it is by no means the only form of literature to be valued.

SERIES BOOKS

Many boys and girls collect, borrow and read series books throughout childhood, even books that are well above their actual reading ability. Series books, with their predictable themes and familiar characters, often provide security for less confident and able readers. Readers know that the books will be interesting and accessible, and many readers move on to more substantial reading. For me, such books belong to the world of play and playmaking. Reading them is a way of belonging to the playgroup.

Such series as The Hardy Boys and Nancy Drew have remained popular with children in the middle years. Children enjoy the familiar plot structures and take comfort in the stock heroes. Peer groups have their own power in determining what children will want to read, and adults must recognize this if they hope to influence the reading materials selected by this group. By providing books that are similar in theme, yet of stronger artistic merit, adults can bring young readers gently to an awareness of other appropriate novels. They can begin building the literary foundation of future readers.

Some teachers create units with these series where students analyze and deconstruct the patterns inherent in them. Doing this may help bridge the gaps between home and school, but not if the agenda is to minimize the books' worth or trivialize them. I prefer to have a shelf in the room where children can share and exchange the books as they need to, allowing their outside interests inside the school frame.

MAGAZINES

If you walk into a news store that sells magazines, you may be as amazed as I was at the sheer number of them, many directed at teens, teen girls or teen boys. Others are distributed through the mail. There is no better marker of the differences in life reading and school reading than these. How are we who work in schools supposed to accommodate this print resource, an important literacy factor in so many of their lives? Even as a free reading enterprise, some schools have banned magazines from the library.

Worrying about what boys read isn't new. In the just-published 50th anniversary edition of her classic novel, Henry Huggins, *author Beverly Cleary notes that she wrote the book in response to her difficulty in finding interesting books for boys when she was a children's librarian.*

"There was very little on the library shelves those boys wanted to read," Cleary recalled. "Finally, one of them burst out, 'Where are the books for kids like us?' Where, indeed. There weren't any."

MH-18, *a Fall 2000 spin-off of* Men's Health, *is one of the only male teen lifestyle magazines out there. According to Stan Zukowski, the senior editor at MH-18, the goal of the magazine is "to deliver fitness, health and relationship advice to teen guys, ages 13 to 18. It's a service magazine. It's light on the fluff. You come to this magazine to learn something." Zukowski believes that the magazine industry is only now targeting male teens because "suddenly, people are realizing teen guys read. They won't read a 2000-word story, but they will watch TV and pick it up and read bits in between. It took a while to realize how they read."*

How can we promote literacy and not notice or support what young people read? Could we use some less explicit magazines (in a select and limited way) to help them examine and critically consider what they are reading? If we see literacy as a set of much-needed life skills, we will need to apply these thinking strategies to *everything* we read, not only to what our culture determines as literature.

Those books are too slow for these guys. They were looking for books about wolves on motorcycles. That's when I got the idea for 'The Time Warp Trio.' I wanted to give them something that appeals to them, with action, cliffhanger endings, fast dialogue.

Jon Scieszka

Although I was a reader, I did not associate books with writing. I liked to look at pictures of writers, and none of the writers whom I was studying in school had any relation to anything I knew as being real. They were all, as far as I knew, dead. Those who weren't dead were probably English, which meant the same thing to me. That year I also discovered a book that alluded to sex. It was one of my better finds for the year.

From Bad Boy: A Memoir
by Walter Dean Myers

The question was "What is your favorite book?" The Grade 3 students wanted to have the choice to include their friends as well as their family as part of the survey and so the investigation began. They each surveyed five people and after gathering the data, we analyzed the results together.

We discovered that boys and girls like to read different types of books. Favorite topics and books for boys included dinosaurs, Pokemon, Captain Underpants,

The Magic Tree House books, Arthur books, sports-related books, Harry Potter books, and Dr. Seuss books. Some boys said they like short and easy books, and some boys said they like hard books because they're interesting. A few mentioned that they enjoyed scary books and reading over the Internet. The Harry Potter books they mentioned were books that their Grade 7 reading buddies or parents were reading to them. Several students mentioned that they would like to have a "Leap Frog" interactive "book."

Girls chose different books, such as fairy tales, Barbie books, Mary Kate and Ashley books, Disney books (The Lion King, The Little Mermaid), Winnie the Pooh, books about dogs, and Blue's Clues books. Many said that they watch the cartoons on television and then look for the books. Some of the books were read to them by their parents.

Michelle Kuleka

At age 16 and 17 at high school in Montreal, I read War and Peace, learning how to anticipate and skip over the philosophy sections to follow the story. After this I fell in love with Dostoevsky and read everything I could find.

At 18 I immersed myself in McGill University's collection of diaries and memoirs written by participants in the Seven Years' War in Canada, instead of

studying for my Engineering courses . . .

At about 24 or 25 I read the Icelandic Burnt Njal's Saga. A few weeks later I realized I had become so obsessed with the book that I had retold the whole story to everyone I knew. I did a mid-twenties reassessment of my life, and concluded that I was living vicariously through my books, rather than living my own life. In reaction I borrowed a scale and sold the whole collection to my friends at $1/lb. My only later regrets were a few otherwise unavailable art resource books, such as one about the construction of wooden churches in sixteenth century Russia.

Now I read all the time: mostly work-related papers, though I have a very low tolerance and really only scan for sense. But I am easily sucked into the escape of binge reading. I try to limit novels to times when I can afford to ignore all else. I just worked my way through Patrick O'Brian's Napoleonic series. I recently enjoyed Cod by Mark Kurlansky, travel books by Redmond O'Hanlan, the Indonesian Biru Quartet by Pramoedya Ananta Toer, and a mystery series with a D.A. called Carp. I have an ongoing relationship with the Encyclopedia Britannica, tending to just pick up a volume at random and read, though I avoid the scientific details.

David Powell

5. This computer is running out of memory!

Acknowledging the impact of computer technology on boys' literacy

The disparities between the electronic plugged-in bedroom and the traditional school contribute to the alienation that many boys feel about what goes on in their classrooms. That raises a question. How can we build on their digital literacies as we reconceptualize how to teach reading and writing?

This issue reminds me of an incident. On a visit to a Grade 4 classroom, I read aloud to the students several poems about nature from my book *Impressions of Nature.* As usual, I was impressed with their young minds' abilities to connect their lives and imaginations to the images created by the writers and the artists. I would listen carefully to the spontaneous ideas that the work generates, and then help frame students' thoughts so that we could find more meanings together. And at the end of the session, I felt quite pleased with myself.

Then, a young boy asked me if I had heard of the woman who lived in a tree. When I said I had not, he told us a bit about her. He then suggested that he would pull some information together and courier it to me! He was eight years old. Three days later, a package arrived at my desk, containing a complete dossier of articles and photographs about this woman, along with a table of contents, a summary the boy had written from the printouts, his reflections on the event, and a collage he had made from the colored photos downloaded from different Web sites.

Welcome to the digital world of information!

In Finland, home of Nokia, all sixth grade children have portable telephones, but they don't just talk to each other; they use their keypads as computer keyboards, and they communicate through typing messages—"texting with each other." The most interesting aspect of this information phenomenon, however, is that it is predicted in two years, all of the seven-year-olds there will be doing the same, using palm-sized devices to make the whole process simpler. Beyond that, the news media showed a clip of a school in China using "paperless books," the boys and girls each with a hand-held screen print device. What does this mean for young people in the future—and are we preparing them well enough?

One of the great appeals of computers for boys is that they are intrinsically motivating and students can set their own goals. It is easy for educators to forget how rapidly computers and technology have become a part of the repertoire of tools available to us in our schools; it is equally easy to forget the benefits that these tools are able to provide. For many boys, who have a natural predilection for solitary, fact-based activities, computer use is a natural and comfortable tool for learning. However, at the same time, computers can prove to be an obstacle for them in their literacy learning given that information on the Web is frequently inaccurate and at times incorrect.

That girls and boys come to technology in different ways has been proven in various studies. Although girls have narrowed the gender gaps in math and science, technology remains dominated by boys. According to Lanius (1999), "girls consistently rate themselves lower than boys on computer ability, and boys exhibit higher self-confidence and a more positive attitude about computers than girls do." As well, there is evidence that boys use computers outside of school more often than girls do. We know from research on gender and literacy that boys prefer resources (books, magazines, Web sites) that favor facts over fiction. The Web contains an endless frontier of facts on all manner of topics! What is more, boys respond to the factual and multimodal (written, image, sound, animation modes) nature of the Internet.

As parents and educators, we should be aware of the use of technology in the classroom. For instance, students, especially boys, should not take Web pages at face value. They should be active viewers and consult multiple sources—CD-ROMs, reference books, CD encyclopedias, newspapers, and the Internet—when researching and writing classroom assignments. They should adopt a more active, self-directed, and constructive perspective on Web-based materials.

Studies of gender and learning show that while many boys prefer objective information, many girls prefer connecting with what they are learning. Generally speaking, girls prefer to work with their peers in groups while boys opt more to work on their own. As a result, the use of technological tools, like computers, befits boys' learning habits. Yet, computer use hinders development in areas that boys should and need to cultivate, such as collaborative learning and having a meta-awareness of texts they read. To encourage students, particularly boys, to become more discerning and critical in their use of the Internet, we need to teach them to be active and critical in their use of multimedia.

Students need to have a critical lens on Web pages, bearing in mind some of the questions that Ron Jobe and Mary Dayton-Sakari cite in their book, *INFO KIDS: How to Use Nonfiction to Turn Reluctant Readers into Enthusiastic Learners*: "Is a site up to date? Who created a site? What is the expertise of the person entering the data? Is a site accurate or correct? How much time is spent hunting for information?" Boys should be mindful of these types of questions and vigilant that they do not get lost in cyberspace or incorporate inaccurate or incorrect information into their written work.

Students today think of themselves as programmers, as interface designers when they read and generate texts on the computer. They interweave such modes as written text, sounds, animation, and perhaps even video to enhance their assignments. Computers can also be used to visualize abstract concepts or to solve problems. As a result, we can no longer view the texts we use during literacy teaching as primarily written or linguistic—they are made up of images, of sounds, of movement. The texts that students read and enjoy at home are print *and* electronic. Our choice of texts in the classroom needs to reflect the multimodality seen on the Web and in CD-ROM to appeal to boys' reading habits.

Students who are living inside the new technological literacies need to do more than know how to work the bits and pieces: they need to see the role of these digital movements in shaping the world they live in. Technology is part of a larger set of social relationships, like a spider web touching everything in their lives.

For those of us who are anxious to introduce boys to critical perspectives of the media, we need to be careful not to establish a negative barrier against the popular culture and media, another "us and them" war. Popular texts, books, magazines, TV shows, films, CDs and computer games can reinforce or challenge gender norms. If we accept these resources as influential in the lives of youngsters, we can carefully engage students in looking at them through a critical, but never cynical lens. I have no doubt that my son has new and different technological abilities that I will never acquire. He is equipped to "think" computers, with a new set of literacy skills.

Technology provides an ideal vehicle for boys to become more acquainted with literacy and being literate. In the on-line world, they can safely play around with technology without worrying about their image.

The key point, as with printed texts, is making technology one's own. For both boys and girls, computer skills should pivot more on building and designing than on being passive in relation to technology. Although gender clearly plays a role in relation to technology, we need to create new spaces for thinking of literacy in terms of the multimodal nature of texts that children read, use, and produce.

Jennifer Rowsell notes that "the emergence of new media opens up children's communicational landscape with new, burgeoning modes of communication. We have witnessed our students' steady mastery of such standard practices as clicking, cutting and pasting, creating and updating web pages, and even writing text codes. These practices are so tacit to their lives that they hardly give them a second thought. Practices such as these have been psychologized by our students and have become fundamental to the reading and writing process."

The following table demonstrates gender differences in how boys and girls respond to books and computer technology.

QUESTION: If you had a choice which one of these things would you do?	Boys	Girls	Total
a) watch your favorite TV program	24.16%	34.88%	29.91%
b) play a new computer game	48.99%	20.35%	33.64%
c) read a really good book	16.78%	42.44%	30.53%

Source: *Contemporary Juvenile Reading Habits*, by Kim Reynolds (Roehampton Institute, 1994)

Only 16.78 percent of boys in all age groups would prefer to read a book, whereas 42.44 percent of girls would prefer to read a book rather than watch television.

Jon Scieszka, the author of popular books for boys, has created a Web site as a forum for boys to discuss issues related to their reading and writing. Scieszka created GUYS READ (www.guysread.com) as a literacy initiative for boys. In his words, it is "a literacy program to give boys more of a say with books they will want to read; a literacy program to help boys become better readers, better students, better guys."

Jay is sitting at his desk in his room creating a picture of his computer—inner workings, keyboard, and a message in tiny letters on screen that reads: "Once upon a time a boy wrote a story about a computer . . ." He is wearing track pants with "olympic" written on the side, a shirt emblazoned with "I danced at the Met," and a racing cap with "Coca Cola" glued to it. He is drawing and writing with a pencil labeled HB sporting a motif from Pembroke Publishers.

D. B.

The gummy gives me a look, like he wants to memorize me or something. "Remembering things is very important to a writer. Before you can put it down on paper, you have to remember what happened."

"Put what down on paper? What are you spewing, huh?" He takes a piece of paper from the pile of stuff he's trying to hide in the crate. The paper is covered with small black marks. I hold it up close to my eyes, to see if there's anything hidden there, inside the paper, but to me the marks look like the footprints of bugs.

"I used to use a voicewriter like everybody else, but it got ripped off," Ryter explains. "So I went back to basics. I write down each word by hand, like they did in backtimes. Primitive, but it works."

I go, "But what's the point? What are you putting inside your 'book'?"

Ryter looks at me for a while before he says, "Sorry, son, but that's between me and myself. I can tell you this much: My book is the work of a lifetime."

"You're wasting your time," I tell him. "Nobody reads books anymore." Ryter nods sadly. "I know. But someday that may change. And if and when it does, they'll want stories—experiences—that don't come out of a mindprobe needle. People will want to read books again, someday."

"'They'?" I go. "Who do you mean.?"

"Those who will be alive at some future date," he says.

From The Last Book in the Universe
by Rodman Philbrick

First launched in the United States four years ago, the IBM technology day camp has since opened in 24 locations worldwide, playing host to more than 1,000 girls at IBM facilities from Australia to Malaysia —all of which are fully funded, with no cost to the participants.

The global attempt to halt the mass exodus of girls from science points to an industry that's trying desperately to deepen the pool of high-tech talent and make way for a massive influx of women.

Isabel Teotonio, in The Toronto
Star, Saturday, August 24, 2002

Technology, like stone tablets, quills and biros and the printing press, is a tool of literacy, not literacy itself. It is vital that we develop students' ways of critically deconstructing the texts that they read on the computer screen. Very often information on the Internet is not sourced. Was it all written by Bill Gates? And can our students recognize the value, the bias, the capitalist conformity, which spews out of the computer, just as we require them to in books, journals, manuals and the like? How should work printed directly from the computer be assessed?

Apart from the challenge of developing literate computer users, there is a final problem for us: U.S. researchers have identified a new generation of visual learners who are accustomed to watching hours of television and who put together reality in 20 second grabs. How do our current classroom literacy strategies accommodate these sorts of learners, and is this where we are failing to meet the needs of our current generation of boys?

Jacqueline Lyons,
deputy principal

My mentor child is a Grade 5 boy named Fabio. This year is a special year for Fabio because it is the first year he has been integrated into a regular class. Before this, he was in a health class due to his medical problem.

Although Fabio was born in Canada, he is an ESL student. His parents have emigrated from Portugal and do not speak English to him at home. He also lives with his grandparents who speak Portuguese to him. Fabio has a 20-year-old brother who seems to be pretty supportive and has hooked him on to the world of computers.

This brings me to his interests. There are two things that Fabio absolutely loves to do. One is playing games on his computer. This helped me pique some of his interest in writing since we had the use of three computers in the classroom. Fabio and his partner wrote of this interest during a readers theatre lesson we did with the class. The other hobby Fabio has is collecting hockey and baseball cards. He doesn't really follow the sports much, but he enjoys collecting. This helped us with our math activities.

Student teacher

Derrick's self-esteem was very low; his peers often chided him about his inability to read as well as they could and he was involved in many verbal and physical fights because of that. He was in the lowest reading group and was fully aware of this fact. Once, I heard him refer to his group as the "stupid group." Obviously, he needed some activities that would make him feel like a successful reader, so I tried to make our sessions together as entertaining as possible. He seemed to enjoy himself and quickly became very comfortable with me . . .

Probably the most effective activity that we did was writing a story that he had taped, and publishing it (writing it on the computer and giving it pictures and a cover) and then reading it first to his teacher and then to the whole class. He was very proud of himself.

In working with Derrick, I found that motivation was important in helping him become more literate and a crucial motivator is success. I also learned that reading becomes easier if there is no pressure placed on the child. Our conferences were in an informal and relaxed atmosphere, and I think that made Derrick more comfortable with me which helped him stay motivated with the tasks.

Student teacher

How can we begin to work towards equity in schools and classrooms? One way is for teachers to observe their interactions with students. When every teacher in one school videotaped a lesson and then shared it with colleagues, many surprised themselves when they noticed how they answered or called upon boys and girls, how often and for what reasons. Your school might make this an excellent professional development activity.

In a U.S. survey of 3000 students in Grades 4 to 10, most of the boys as well as the girls said that teachers preferred girls. That finding no doubt relates to the fact that girls typically want to please the teacher, while boys want to impress their peers. What would a similar survey at your school discover? Consider implementing one.

William Pollack's *Real Boys* is an extremely useful resource in sorting out many of the conflicting theories of what we want boys to become in our society and of how we should go about effecting change. Although some educators see his work as supporting the traditional goals of male roles, he himself talks about understanding the "Boy Code" and breaking through its limited views. Pollack has helped me to look carefully at the culture of boyhood and to listen to what boys have to say.

Does your school unintentionally support or even strengthen the "Boy Code"? What could be done to move into an acceptance of a more diverse set of masculine behaviors and attitudes that reflect the best and most positive elements of the boy culture?

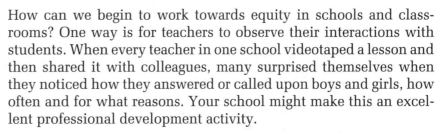

In *Reading the Difference*, edited by Myra Barrs and Sue Pidgeon, 12 teachers and researchers offer valuable insights into gender and literacy from their own classroom experiences. Each of the articles would work well as a shared reading opportunity with teachers from a division in a school. After reading and discussing the chapter, the group could brainstorm ways to focus on gender issues in their own classrooms by conducting similar observations. My graduate class of experienced teachers did just that and the findings from their students gave us so much to consider and rethink about how we work with boys and girls.

In *Boys, Literacy and Schooling*, the authors present a case for literacy teaching as a transformative practice for implementing gender and literacy reform. They outline the factors that intersect with gender that have an impact on the kinds of reading and writing events that boys and girls will likely experience. They advocate alternative, multiple and literate performances of school-based masculinity. How do members of your staff view these goals? In your own school or in your classroom, what examples can you share of student responses (written and oral) that demonstrate a similar approach to texts? What types of activities could you implement that might change stereotypical behaviors and responses?

The work on emotional intelligence fits into the scheme of why so many boys have trouble with reflective responses to reading, and in articulating and expressing their feelings in their writing. In *Raising Cain: Protecting the Emotional Life of Boys*, authors Michael Thompson and Ian Kindlon share their stories of boys "threatened by emotional complexities, unversed in the subtleties of emotional language and expression. They lash out or withdraw emotionally." They feel that most boys are ill prepared for the challenges in becoming emotionally healthy adults, aided and abetted by a culture that discourages emotional responses in boys and favors them in girls. These boys lack the emotional vocabulary for both recognizing and naming their feelings, as well as missing the ability to read the emotions of others. Too many boys meet the emotional pressures of adolescence with "anger, aggression and emotional withdrawal."

Piggybook by Anthony Browne has brought me fascinating responses every time I have read it to various groups. It is the story of a working wife and mother who abandons her family for a while due to their lack of support in helping with the household chores. The husband and sons gradually turn into pigs, snuffling and grubbing for food. All is resolved when they repent and promise to help; she returns and fixes the family car.

In Chicago, after listening, a man tearfully announced that he was from a family of eight kids and his mother had never sat down with them at the dinner table for a meal; she had just served them. In a Grade 6 classroom, a boy was very angry that the fictional mother had left her family, but a girl challenged him to prove how things would have changed for this character if she had not taken such drastic action. This book talk went on for 40 minutes, with each comment building a clearer scenario of possibilities for family behaviors.

Consider having children examine male/female roles in different books they have read and chart the paths each main character followed in attempting to bring about equity. Was there resolution or indicators of what might change in their lives?

Older students (Grades 6 to 8) could observe children's play at recess and note occurrences of gender-specific activities, including those events where both boys and girls participate. These notes could form the basis for interesting discussions.

B. Helping Boys Become Print Powerful

6. I will never learn to read.

Providing support for boys who are at risk in literacy

We know that most non-readers, unmotivated readers, reluctant readers, and limited readers can all change with the right set of conditions. We know stories from those who teach adults who are illiterate how their students eventually become print powerful. We hear from teachers who work with youngsters in remedial reading classes of the great strides many of the students make with guidance and instruction. And we listen to the stories of those who struggled with reading—some of them now teachers and writers—who, with the help of someone who understood the reading process, gained membership in the literacy club.

In *Supporting Struggling Readers and Writers*, the authors have summarized the factors often found in readers experiencing difficulties in reading and writing. Some are youngsters just learning to read for the first time; some have struggled for years and, for a variety of reasons, have failed to make sense of print. The boys we are talking about may represent combinations of these factors:

- some children (about 6 percent) are cognitively challenged and unable ever to learn to read;
- some have physical or mental disabilities;
- some have visual or hearing difficulties;
- some have limited proficiency in English, or are from homes in which a nonstandard dialect of English is spoken;
- some have a history of preschool language impairment, or parents who had difficulty learning to read;
- some are faced with attention deficit hyperactivity disorder (ADHD);
- some live in poor neighborhoods;
- some attend schools in which classroom practices are deemed ineffective; and
- still others have given up on reading after a few years, lacking the word power and fluency that proficient readers bring to print texts.

Unfortunately for these struggling readers, the act of reading facilitates the development of being able to understand a wide variety of

Jay will eventually go to bed and read until I declare lights out from the next room.

He will then, as usual, pull the sheet over his head, turn on the flashlight and continue reading in his secret world. I will ten minutes later go into his room, remove the book from his sleeping hands, shut off the flashlight and kiss him goodnight. He will sleep with a smile on his face, as I have forgotten tonight's bath.

Jay has learned to read. In spite of his dad, his teachers, his friends, his social life. On his own.

He also swims—feebly, but with future potential. The water will always welcome him because he has begun to understand it, to live inside it, even to travel under it. He will always sense the freedom that comes when one floats on sea alone. Like print, I hope.

D. B.

I remember a teacher once telling me about a hired hand who worked on their family's farm. Each month, he received a letter from a woman friend in a faraway city, and because he couldn't read, her father would take the chap into the front parlour, close the sliding doors, and read the love letter aloud to him. Then the hired hand would dictate his response, and the farmer would transcribe the letter for him. And all the while, the teacher remembered, she could hear the sobs of sadness from the man through the parlour doors.

D. B.

texts. As they read, children learn more word meanings, experience an understanding of how print works, and as a result, learn to read even better. Children who read less, who read slowly and often without enjoyment, will have trouble growing as readers, and will soon experience their limitations with different texts. In learning to read, "more is better."

English as a Second Language (ESL) students benefit from literacy strategies that build on their oral ability and extend their speaking and listening vocabularies. They can bring their existing language competency to their print experiences. Since many ESL students are fluent readers and writers in their home languages, they can also build on this strength. Research suggests that those who are beginning readers may benefit from literacy instruction in their home language.

NON-READERS

I would like to focus on two categories of non-readers in this book: young beginning readers who may be having difficulties, and boys (and girls) in the junior and intermediate years who lack success in reading and writing and see themselves as non-readers.

If we don't help each of these groups early in their school careers, then in high school, they will be unable to participate in most curriculum subjects, often forced to hide their inabilities in unhelpful ways. They will become, in Cris Tovani's term, *fake readers*, or eventually dropouts. Such students have no intellectual involvement with the text; they rely on summaries by the teacher, copying what others say; they quickly grow frustrated by a lengthy or complex selection, waiting for the teacher to tell them what to think.

We need to remember that some students demonstrate different behaviors and attitudes towards different types of texts, depending on the context of the experience—the expectations, the interest, the social situation. Sometimes, they *are* readers—it depends greatly on what they are asked to read. When we claim that boys don't read, are we really meaning that boys don't read what we *want* them to read?

An Australian study reveals that girls with learning difficulties are more likely to react with anxiety and withdrawal, while boys are more likely to act aggressively. It also reports that the resulting school behavior problems in boys are more likely to lead to labeling and remedial classes. In several studies on children diagnosed with dyslexia, researchers found twice as many boys as girls identified, when in reality teachers were mistaking behavioral problems for reading problems. Many boys have trouble sitting still at their desks. They are more prone to ADHD which causes impulsive and combative behavior, and difficulty concentrating. On the other hand, girls with ADHD have difficulty concentrating, but are much less restless and disruptive. Since boys do come to reading more slowly than girls, they are often misdiagnosed, and teacher and parent expectations about their potential are lowered.

> *Many boys were floundering because verbal instructions given by teachers were way beyond their auditory capacities to process them. Twenty percent of six-year-old children cannot process verbal information beyond an eight-word sentence. When teachers give verbal instructions using sentences longer than that, a proportion of the children will lose much of what they are being told, start acting out and getting into trouble.*
>
> *It's a problem which could be easily rectified with teacher training. Our study showed that just getting teachers to slow down their instructions, shortening them and maintaining eye contact and waiting for compliance, had strong positive effects on children's learning progress and behavior—especially with boys.*
>
> *Dr. Ken Rowe*

Jay just completed his first complex jigsaw puzzle (a G.I. Joe Action Scene). He spent three hours uninterrupted finishing it. I wonder what relationship this event has to reading—filling in details, seeing the whole while finding the parts. I dislike doing such puzzles and yet took satisfaction and delight in his sticking with and completing the task. Perhaps seeing this evidence of his growth in both concept and patience generates my feelings.

D. B.

Researchers at Southampton University's centre for language and education reported on a two-year project focused on nine seven-year-olds at four schools. They found that boys, when faced with the knowledge that they were poor readers, were less likely to want to improve. Boys who were slow in reading avoided fiction that was "proficiency graded" and tended to go for non-fiction texts with plenty of pictures when given a choice. "Non-fiction texts allow weaker boy readers to escape others' judgements about how well they read or how competent they are. They enable them to maintain self-esteem in their peer group," said Gemma Moss, author of the report. She suggested that boys be encouraged to read fiction texts as opposed to "pandering more to boys' interests." Boys use illustrated non-fiction books to mask their reading difficulties (*Guardian*, July 7, 1999).

One researcher interviewed several mothers of fourth grade boys who were concerned by their sons' decreased interest in reading. It became evident though that these boys were reading as much as before, but were reading different types of materials, for example, newspapers, baseball cards, magazines and manuals. The mothers were actually observing their sons being socialized to a form of literacy; the real concern was that this was different from their concept of literacy.

Boys with difficulty in reading need to experience what successful literacy events feel like, to know that there is hope for recovery and that they will be supported in their struggle to grow towards independence. They need to see themselves as readers and writers. Very few are unable to master literacy; therefore, we will need to recognize and help many different types of struggling readers and writers, to find out what they can do and build on their competencies, no matter how limited. That will enable them to move forward and recognize that they are indeed improving.

Boys need to be provided with the following:

- uninterrupted silent reading times;
- opportunities to listen to you read aloud and tell stories;

Jay's tiny fingers know when to hold a book. His eyes can follow the pages as grown-up voices breathe life into the words. He began with the words he required and those words had to be full of meaning. He knew his name on Christmas presents, restaurant signs, games and television shows. He never was afraid of print.

D. B.

- guided reading times for attending closely to the meanings and the functions of different genres of texts.

They will also need occasions for talking to others in meaningful ways about what they have read (perhaps through dialogue journals or conferences). They will need to constantly hear about new books and other print resources—significant motivation for finding new selections to increase their reading repertoires.

Boys will need to act upon what they have read, to engage with the ideas and the language they have struggled to understand, so that their comprehension expands and their word power increases. Most of all, though, they need to feel that they *own* the reading, that the experience was worthwhile, and that it is now part of their world knowledge and their personal literacy life. They need to feel that reading matters to them.

Many of us (teachers, teacher-librarians and parents) are guilty of missing opportunities for reading as participants ourselves and as models for our children. Often, we are seen as self-designated non-readers, and our children are quick to notice that print time is missing from much of our lives as well. We need to recognize that our own reading lives matter, or what will our children and students think? How can we make our print experiences visible? How can we model what we want young people to value?

RELUCTANT READERS

Reluctant readers are children who can read, but for whatever reason, don't. They may be boys who still feel inadequate as readers compared to their siblings or to other, more proficient readers in the class. Often, they have been through remedial situations, special programs, or commercial drill kits, but they have missed the literacy imperative, the internalized motivation, to read. As teachers and parents, we can help these boys; there are strategies and techniques that have a high success rate with discouraged and frustrated youngsters.

We cannot group all reluctant readers together, for there are many different reasons for their difficulties, many stumbling blocks to their growing as readers: their background experiences; how they feel about themselves as learners; their interests; the context of the classroom (the teacher's skills and attitudes, the resources, the pressures of curriculum). I like the following categories of reluctant readers as developed by Beers:

- dormant (they like to read, but often do not make the time to do it);
- uncommitted (do not like to read, but may read in the future); or
- unmotivated (do not like to read and do not ever expect to change their minds).

Beers explains that even proficient and motivated readers become "dormant" at times: on weekends, during holidays, or after a major project. As well, unmotivated readers may see reading time as skill and drill, rather than as a satisfying and pleasurable activity.

For boys who are reluctant readers, who don't find reading easy, enjoyable or worthwhile, we need to revise our means of dealing with them. We should move towards strategies for involving them in finding reasons for reading other than we demand that they read (although structured time and expectations that reading will occur are part of the solution).

- For these readers especially, independent reading time during school hours is a necessity for enhancing reading abilities and for encouraging a positive attitude towards books and reading. Providing suitable resources is the first hurdle; then, we need to support the silent reading of the text by these boys, sitting nearby or chatting quietly at appropriate checkpoints to clarify what is happening in the story.

- Reluctant readers also need successful experiences with literature circles, where they focus on the themes and issues—the big ideas as well as the words and structures—of the best books for young people. The groups should be of mixed ability, with the children selecting the books they want to read from the classroom or library collections. We may have to assist these readers with their choices. A wide range of suitable and appropriate books, or selections in anthologies, is important, so that we can accommodate the various stages of literacy development in our classrooms. (See Recommended Books for Boys pages 117–125.) Sometimes, we can arrange to have those less-able readers listen to the book on tape beforehand, or have it read aloud to them by an older book buddy, so that they can enter a group discussion as full-fledged members.

- We need to model for and demonstrate with these children the way in which we take part in literary discussions, encouraging their participation through prompts and questions during the talk time, modeling appropriate behavior with our own responses and inviting these students into the conversation. When these readers in difficulty reveal that they, too, have ideas and thoughts about the text and its connections to the world we share, and when they begin to adopt main roles in the discussion, then we can see authentic evidence of their literacy growth.

- We need to help reluctant readers think about what they have read through a variety of response activities. For example, as they connect their reading with their writing, they are learning about both aspects of literacy, strengthening their understanding of the text and making connections with their own worlds of meaning. As they participate in building graphic organizers in the form of webs and charts, they can often see the relationships between the characters in a story or the facts in an information text. The computer can be such a help to these students as they see their words take shape and their ideas appear organized.

READERS WITH ATTENTION DEFICIT DISORDER (ADD)

I enjoyed reading the two books about Joey Pigza by Jack Gantos. Most of us have taught a boy like Joey: "I am how I am because I was born wired, and my dad, Carter Pigza, was born wired, and I followed right behind them. It's as if our family tree looks like a set of high-voltage wires strung across a field from one steel tower to the next."

No matter how hard Joey tries, something seems to go wrong, even with the help of his "meds." Finally, after his constant off-the-wall behavior, he is sent to the "special-ed" centre downtown, and he finds help.

Boys, like Joey, need to become readers and writers, and the road is uphill all the way for them—and for the teachers and parents. I would use whatever I could find that they want to read, and have them write about what they care about in short, carefully programmed units of time, so that they feel like real readers and writers as often as possible.

The number of boys, like Joey, identified as having ADD with a neuro-developmental problem has remained constant over several years. Some researchers suggest that many children show similar patterns of behavior because social and environmental changes have disturbed their capacity to regulate themselves. Many boys live in complex worlds, in a variety of family situations, with a much different set of tensions than in my childhood. A large number of boys today are labeled ADD, but not diagnosed as such by specialists. Although no one denies the difficulties and disruptions that boys such as Joey cause, they might become proficient readers and writers with more effective literacy programs and resources. We will need to build support for our efforts in a crowded classroom.

"The idea that some kinds of talent may be the flip side of what is usually considered a disability is something that I think should be contemplated more often in education. Reading is certainly important in our modern world, but it seems to me that there is enough variability in the kinds of jobs people can have that perhaps we could afford to try to teach to children's strengths rather than their weaknesses. Often when children do poorly in reading, they end up spending more time than their classmates working on their "reading problem." I would be more inclined to try to figure out what those kids are really good at and let them forge ahead in those subjects, as long as functional competence in reading could be achieved."

From Vision and Art:
The Biology of Seeing,
by Margaret Livingstone

when I first started reading I usedto try to read a long word like Information for example.I used to need help from my teacher and my parents. when I started as a reader I did't relly like it till I read Castoway:It's about 6 kids Instead of boot camp,tehey become Castaways. It was a 269 paged book I thought it was very Iteresting book.one of the things and poeple that help me was my teacher,Mrs,Conner last year in grade 3 Mrs,Conner would stay after shcool & read with me.

Reading is a past time now I read when I want to,where I want to,not because I half too.In my last shcool reading wasn't a big thing,but in Mrs,Conner's reading is evrything.There was also some problemes I had For example I used to get nervise reading in front of the hole studen't body.I used to mess words up even The I would ither skip by axadint or stuter.I would become shy & unable to speek.Evrybody would lalf I & would run of the stage inbarest sad. I felt that reading made me happy &it also cleard my mind so I could work.Reading

takes my mind off things that bother me. My teacher would let me stay in if I watd to,now reading is fun & injoyble.

Miles

I once had a student who began Grade 2 with me, but was functioning at a Kindergarten level. He had difficulty with reading and as a matter of fact could not read the washroom door in order to determine if it said boys or girls. I remember thinking how could it have gone on this long without someone saying something, a parent or a teacher. How come nobody fought for him? I was determined that he receive help for some of his difficulties. So he began to receive Reading Recovery instruction and was caught in time as he began to have many successes with the one-on-one reading instruction. In the classroom, I planned a totally separate program and his language instruction was tailored for his reading abilities. I searched for reading books at his level and spent at least 15 minutes a day just hearing him read. He looked so forward to that time and I enjoyed it as well. I'll never forget when he said, "Miss Curatolo, thanks for not giving up on me."

Primary teacher

I was never the best reader in school. I can't remember clearly, but I think that I was in the middle reading group. I do recall that I was always a slow reader, preferring to linger over pictures and words and letting my imagination run with the ideas that they conjured up in my mind. On more than one report card, it was noted that I liked to daydream. I blame books for that!

Our family bought a piano when I was in Grade 4 and I was the first of my siblings to take piano lessons. In addition to learning to "read" music, I was also inspired by the stories of musical composers. I read books about Chopin, Mendelssohn, Beethoven, Mozart and Bach. I was particularly excited to discover that all of these artists were very proficient and creative at a very young age. I wanted to be proficient and creative!

But something happened in Grade 5 that affected my life as a reader. In November of that year, I received my first pair of glasses. I had been under the care of an eye specialist from a very young age, but it wasn't until I was 10 that I was given my first prescription. It was wonderful to be able to see the world in such finely tuned

detail. I often wonder whether my vivid imagination was really compensation for not being able to see the real world as clearly as others.

While the eyeglasses allowed me to bring the world around me into focus, I recall losing an interest in books. Come to think of it, I can't remember a single book that I read for pleasure after Grade 5. Oh, I read for school and in school, but admittedly, it wasn't something that I found enjoyable. In fact, even throughout high school and university, I found written material very difficult to begin, and even more difficult to complete. Reading was physically tiresome and, at times, painful.

It wasn't until I was scheduled for eye surgery in my second year of university that I began to put some of the pieces together. It was explained to me at that time that very early on in my life I had developed a condition known as strabismus. Quite simply, both of my eyes worked independently of one another and focused on objects separately. As a result, as I grew up, one of my eyes had become stronger and more dominant than the other. The addition of eyeglasses (and later, contact lenses) to my life served to bring both of my eyes up to a similar strength. While the world became clearer, the accommodations that I had made early on in my life were now suddenly thrown out of balance. As it turns out, this made reading text very difficult while wearing my glasses.

It took a long time after my eye surgery to figure it out, but I found that reading without my glasses allowed me to achieve a more comfortable balance, greater fluency and much longer reading sessions.

As I write this piece, I look over at the close to 400 books that make up my personal library. A collection of fiction, non-fiction, philosophy, theology, children's literature, technical manuals, professional

journals, books that are unread, books that have been read several times.

Steve Hurley

As a Reading Recovery teacher, I work very closely with students in a one-on-one setting in order to get them to become independent readers and writers. One student that I had been working with was Eric. Eric was accepted into the program in September. The reason I have chosen to write about this student is that the "light has gone on" for Eric. During one of our sessions, Eric was reading a passage from a level 9 book. I think the book was called Little Bulldozer Helps Again. As he was reading it for the first time, he made an error but kept on reading. By the end of the page, he realized his error and said, "Wait a minute." But the way he said this made it quite clear to me that Eric had cracked the code. It sounded more like waaaaaaait a Minnnnnnute! He immediately went back to his error and self-corrected it. As he continued to read, it happened again. I was shocked at the processing that was taking place and the fact that Eric was verbalizing it, almost like he knew that I wanted to hear this (considering most kids do this in their head).

After the lesson, I had to share the news with his teacher. However, this did not come as a shock to her. When I told her the good news she said, "He does that all the time," and that she didn't know why he did it, but that it was quite annoying. So I sat down with his teacher and explained what was going on inside little Eric's mind. At first, she did not agree, so I invited her to come and observe a lesson and show her what I meant. The next day, Eric said "Wait a minute" three times, which helped to prove my point.

Primary teacher

7. This book is too hard!

Letting boys in on the secrets of proficient readers

Jay is such a fine little reader. I don't know how it happened, bit by bit. I suppose, day by day, book by book. We never called it learning to read; we simply read books and everything in sight. Of course it's magic. Run from those who claim it isn't. Find a child who can't read. Become that mature tutor, and locate something he wants to read. It will take time, but we old folks aren't in a hurry. We know that it may not happen by June 29th. What a luxury it can be to eliminate deadlines for childhood growth!

D. B.

This morning, Jay and his friend Marah perused the menu at Shopsy's, deciding upon waffles with syrup, and while waiting for their order, they both read all the local newspaper, looking for events that required persuading parents that they might attend.

D. B.

I remember the reading lessons I taught in my early years as a teacher. I had little, if any, awareness of what "the reading strategies" might be, perhaps because I could already read and had not been aware of how I had mastered this magic process. My methodology consisted of this: "The students read the story (often I hadn't); they read the story out loud one by one, and several times, so that the other children could note (and call out) errors; then they answered tons of questions that I had copied verbatim from the manual."

There is a time and place for every kind of reading: reading for the big picture and reading for details. We need to see how the details fit together to form a whole and move towards sifting essential ideas and synthesizing our final thoughts.

Some boys note details and main ideas, writing them down in notebooks and highlighting them in their textbooks, but are still unable to remember what they were trying to understand. What strategies can we give them for determining what matters in a reading selection, what points will be significant, what details will affect their meaning making?

There is seldom any useful reason for finding the answers to a series of questions that ask students to locate or, even worse, to remember insignificant details from a story or a novel. What we use in constructing meaning are the pieces of information that add to our growing understanding of what we want to find out or need to experience. These details we can't do without; they are pieces of the puzzle necessary to creating the complete picture.

The question has to be: *which* details matter? In my own teaching, I am trying never to ask a student to locate a detail unless that piece of information is necessary for a deeper understanding of what is being explored. Even more important, I want the student to search out the facts necessary for understanding, for supporting an idea or clarifying a point, not to rely on a treasure hunt for details that I determine important.

Lists of predigested and impersonal comprehension questions are no longer part of my life or my classroom teaching. However, manuals for published programs can offer me ideas for giving students thoughtful and deepening literacy strategies. They might also suggest book sets for increasing the reading repertoires of the students or present significant background information for supporting the text.

Of course, I have questions to ask, but they will grow from conversations about the text, from the honest revelations of the students' own concerns, as I try to guide them into deeper interpretations. I try to ask honest questions that are driven by their inquiring dialogue, as I would in a conversation with peers during a book club session, based on my listening to their interactions.

Bear these suggestions about questions in mind.

- We can model and demonstrate how effective questions work, showing the need to listen carefully to others, revisiting points in the text that support a particular comment, and supporting effective student responses.

- Try asking no questions during a text discussion, but note down the ones you might have asked in the past. Consider tape recording a text talk session between you and the children, and play it back to analyze the types of questions you used and the effect they had on your students' contributions.

- Rather than initiating questions, build on the questions and comments of the students by offering open-ended responses after they speak, encouraging further contributions, and helping to focus and deepen the dialogue.

- Consider using prompts rather than recall questions in your interactions with the students. You could do this during group sessions and individual conferences, and in your responses to their reading and writing journals. These prompts can expand or deepen the offerings of the students, helping them to clarify or expand their thoughts, and nudging them into expressing their opinions and ideas. Although we have questions to ask and we need to ask them, we want to teach our students to ask their own, to behave as proficient readers do, framing personal and public questions to promote deeper understanding of the ideas stimulated by the text.

- Separate assessment questions from your text discussions. Clearly stating the purpose of the evaluation activity, whether in practice sessions or in a testing situation, can help students understand the different purposes and learn how to handle both types of events.

BUILDING BACKGROUND KNOWLEDGE

When we are engaged in the act of reading, we make connections constantly as we recall personal experiences, summarize what has happened so far, synthesize information and add it to our constantly expanding mental storehouse, analyze and challenge the author's ideas, and change the organizational schema of our minds. Making connections with what we read is a complex process. When we instruct students to notice, for example, only the words in a text without reading for meaning, we are eliminating all of the other mental connections that educate us as readers.

Our main goal as literacy teachers and as parents must be to help children build bridges between the ideas they are reading and their own lives. We need to help them to access the prior knowledge that is relevant to making meaning with the text, the information that life experience has retained and remembered in the brain, sometimes accompanied by emotional responses or visual images. When we give children a framework for understanding how they can enhance their own reading by activating their own connections, we offer them a reading strategy for life. These connections have been classified as

- text to self: connecting to past experiences and background;
- text to text: connecting to other texts in their lives, and the forms those texts take;
- text to world: connecting to events in the world at large.

Of course, these three general categories interconnect and intersect, but students then have an opening for approaching a text. As they begin to observe, take note of and reflect upon how these connections affect their understanding of a particular text, they can deliberately use each aspect of the connection frame to increase their personal and collective processes of meaning making.

Several factors can increase a child's comprehension, including prior knowledge of the topic, prior exposure to the author's work, or a personal connection to the topic. If a boy is about to read a text, we can often increase his chances of success by providing him with some information that relates to the text, or by reviewing aspects of the text, including chapter heads, supportive visual cues, or unusual vocabulary within the text. This is not to say that we preteach vocabulary; rather, that we acquaint children with the type of terminology they are about to meet in their reading.

In *Wringer*, author Jerry Spinelli examines some masculine myths with a careful eye. The hero can't kill the birds injured in the yearly pigeon shoot by wringing their necks, and this job has been assigned to 11-year-old boys. How the young man deals with this ritualistic failure allows us as readers to confront our own value systems and their conflicts within societal norms.

I have used an excerpt from *Wringer* with teachers at many conferences, and it never fails to elicit personal anecdotes from audience members about their own connection with pigeons—from an uncle who kept them as pets, to weddings where pigeon was served as an entrée. Teachers have e-mailed me their personal pigeon stories from as far away as Saudi Arabia, and from towns next door to where I live. Some of us can share our life stories aloud in an auditorium, while others require the distancing that private writing times provide. Life stories that teachers write can be so useful in helping youngsters to see themselves and those around them as authentic readers and writers. (See Michael Ross's story on page 69.)

If we feel that we are prisoners of a timetable, we can develop units that allow for boys to return to a theme or an issue over several

When pigeons carry stories
The pigeon's eye is like a polished shirt
  button.
The pigeon's eye is orange with a
  smaller black button in the center.
It looks up at him.
It does not blink.
It seems as if the bird is about to
  speak, but it does not.
Only the voices speak:
"Writing it! Writing it! Writing it!
He cannot.
He cannot writing it, nor can he let go.
  He wants to let go, desperately, but
  his fingers are stone.
And the voices chant
"Writing it! Writing it!" and the orange
  eye stares.

From Wringer,
by Jerry Spinelli

days. And if we value a variety of response modes for different learning styles, then we have greater hope of affecting our youngsters in more lasting and significant ways.

Liam nursed a couple weeks past his sixth birthday which is about the world average for weaning, but in North America considered risky behavior. I recall Liam at age 10 or so months sucking at the breast while flipping the pages of a picture book. You could say that he took in reading as a baby takes in milk.

Home schooling is painful or wonderful depending on how you frame it. When I taught 36 Grade 7/8s, I did not take no for an answer. "Here is the work. Now do it." With Liam, I take no for an answer. "Let's scoot down to the beach," says Liam. (We live in the Beaches of Toronto.) "Good idea," I say. "That will be our physical education." And today's 90 minutes of lessons becomes 40. Some say that a home schooling parent can cover the basics of reading, writing, handwriting, and 'rithmetic in 90 minutes or was it 120? I never make 120. Perhaps Veronica does on her shifts.

Today Liam spent about 35 minutes talking on the telephone to his friend Max about the intricacies of Pokemon and Digimon. (Max is nine years old, very bright, and his father home schools him too.) I am proud that Liam can keep up to Max in conversation.

I call Liam's home school the "Huck Finn School for Boys." We learn by moving, we learn by walking. We take up large issues, such as the nature of God, while talking in our bathtub. "How big is an atom bomb?" he asks. "The first one destroyed a city," I say. "That city was full of civilians," I add with some disgust. Talking is our medium as it was for Plato, Socrates, and Aristotle.

Getting Liam to read worries us. We are considering returning him to the regular school system next September for social reasons. Liam is a social being. He must have friends play with him every day. This year we have his friends from last year's JK/SK. They were in JK last year and now are in SK. After morning SK, they can visit in the afternoon.

We have a perfect schedule: talk, play and formal learning in the morning. Play with friends in the afternoons. (We keep school down to a reasonable time frame as do some European countries finishing at 1:00 p.m.) But next year, these friends will be rounded up, interred, and confined to school for a full day. Liam will be lonely and I will be desperate. In September 2002, we must return him to the system, find an alternative school, or increase exponentially our contacts in the home school world.

Will Ellis

J., now in Grade 2, has a history of behavioral and academic difficulties . . . Core French Senior Kindergarten where he produced violent drawings and had severe temper tantrums . . . one where, in addition to the tantrums, he threw chairs and tables. However, it was discovered that J. was suffering from lead poisoning which produces symptoms such as tantrums, nightmares, and Attention Deficit–like behavior. Since this diagnosis and its subsequent treatment, J. has had to "catch up," in an academic sense, to his fellow classmates. He formally attends Learning Centre twice a week, participated in Speech Therapy, and works on literacy at home with his parents.

J. experienced many language difficulties at the beginning of Grade 2. He was an emergent reader who was still struggling to find interest in books. He could identify and name most letters; however, he could not provide the sound that each produces which greatly inhibited his ability to decode. When I first began working with J., he could not decode even the lowest level basal readers on his own. This struggle with words carried into his writing. He labored over the directionality of print (most of his letters and words were written backwards) and those words which he did manage to write were represented by one or two sounds ("WZ" meant "there was" and "RN" meant "dragon," for example). J.'s stories were representative sounds strung together so that each page looked like one lengthy jumble of letters. In addition, he was a very reluctant reader due, in part, to the stigma attached to isolating him for sessions in the Learning Centre, Speech Therapy, and with me.

However, the Learning Centre provided J. with some effective strategies to improve his reading and writing which, in turn, improved his attitude toward these elements of literacy.

Student teacher

Near the end of the program Luke and I read a non-fiction book called Spiders, by Collin Walker. For the first time, I noticed that he was using the phonographemic cueing system to help him with some words such as "silk" and "be." He attacked the words diligently and with genuine interest in deriving their meaning. He also self-corrected his reading twice.

Luke read this book on his own using other cueing systems, including personal experiences with spiders and pictures. I encouraged him to take it home to his mom and read it to her. For the first time in our work together, I felt that Luke was showing signs of using all his knowledge and skills in order to read. I think it was a breakthrough for Luke and we discussed how he felt after completing the book. He felt extreme pride in his hard work and I revealed my elation to him for his conscientious and successful effort.

Student teacher

8. I don't know what this story is about.

Helping boys to deepen and extend comprehension

How can we help boys who are reluctant readers to actively engage with a book? Unless the reader enters the life of that fictional world in some way, how can he move towards an emotional connection with what is going on, and begin to read inside and all around the words to discover and consider the big ideas the author is working with? How will he begin to infer and surmise the events that deepen and add texture to the story's bare bones? Sometimes, keeping a reading journal can move a reluctant reader into a more involved reading of a text.

KEEPING A READING JOURNAL

Reading journals offer strategies for letting students note thoughts and questions as they read, helping them to focus on particular issues or points of information, and record their personal responses. They can keep a list of the books they have read, and they can include sketches or charts that support their responses. The journal is a continual record of their reading responses and of their journey into literacy.

Responding to students' journals allows you to interact with each of them in a literary conversation. Therefore, it is extremely important that you read their responses as an interested person and as a teacher. Be sure to ask them authentic questions and offer genuine comments and opinions, so that your message connects with the reader's response in some way. You can

- pose questions that involve rethinking or rereading;
- share your own experiences as a reader and writer—the authors and books you enjoy;
- question things that you don't understand or that the student has not clarified;
- ask for more information for a different interpretation;
- recommend other authors or titles or genres, or books with similar themes or events;

*I teach a course in children's literature at my college, and over the years, I have built a large collection of fine picture books, poetry anthologies, folk tales and novels. Imagine my chagrin when five-year-old Jay came home from the library having chosen his first picture book—*The Proverbs of Benjamin Franklin. *I tried to read it to him, but the times have changed, the words we use have altered, and the context for the book was too formal and abstract. We finally abandoned it.*

Children need help in becoming book-conscious, learning which ones will be worth the effort of reading, recognizing titles and authors, reading the blurbs on the back covers, and using the cover design as clues to the content. Each week Jay and I select two or three novels that he feels may be appropriate, and one of them becomes his "book of the week." We record the titles of each reading success, and the list itself generates interest and a sense of fulfillment.

D. B.

- have an authentic conversation even if you haven't read the student's book by valuing his responses and acknowledging his thoughts and feelings;
- help the student think more effectively about the text;
- model quality responses with your personal interactions;
- come to know the student in more personal ways and learn more about him or her as a reader, as a writer and as a person;
- gain information about literacy abilities that can be used in mini-lessons and conferences; and
- look for evidence that the student is developing and refining personal knowledge and opinions about reading, discovering new authors and new genres, and gaining self-awareness as a reader and a writer.

Once a week students can write you a letter that summarizes their own responses from a reading journal. They can extend and refine their ideas, expand their understanding of what they have read, and frame their reading by synthesizing and composing their thoughts to you.

Some boys will be surprised, even shocked, to hear how deeply some of their classmates have moved inside their novels.

In this excerpt from Doug's reading journal, you can observe the honest conversation he and his teacher, Nancy Steele, are having. For many boys, these opportunities to engage in reflective and thoughtful writing are few and far between. Dialogue journals offer us valuable learning and teaching moments, especially if our comments reveal that we have read and accepted the student's developing ideas and opinions, and are authentically interested in exploring them further.

Dear Nancy

I've been thinking about the character Cara Mae. When I first heard about her I thought she was a prude. I didn't think she'd be an exciting character, more like one of those stuck up people who thinks she's so cool 'cause she knows all those horse terms. She reminded me of my sister. But she really wasn't stuck up. She had just a lot of inside issues. She appears more confident than she really is and when she finally opens up to Billy he's blown away.

Doug

Dear Doug

I agree. Cara Mae seems to have some trouble showing her true feelings. To me, she is demonstrating the behaviour of a depressed person. Do you think she was? How do you think Billy helped her? I'm wondering if this relationship was a realistic one or just the stuff of some fiction.

Nancy

Dear Nancy

Some people who are depressed just mope around to get pity. They act like they're miserable all the time because they just want to get pity. Cara Mae wasn't really like that. When she got depressed or angry she just disappeared. She just had low self-confidence. Mostly she gets angry with herself if she doesn't do something right. Billy sort of built her up by telling her how great he thought she was. He also made her laugh. I think her romance with Billy is deeper than just a physical thing. Most kids that I know aren't like that. I don't think they'd talk about feelings the way that these two characters did. Still I think that Billy had more effect on his uncle than he did on Cara Mae.

Doug

Dear Doug

I was surprised by your comment about Billy's uncle. I always thought of the uncle's effect on Billy rather than the opposite. Billy's uncle is a lovely, wise and successful man. He owns a store in which he sells Native art and jewelry. He has all the trappings of a good life: a good relationship with his brother, many friends, lots of respect and plenty of money. It's interesting that you think that Billy was so influential in his uncle's life since his uncle wasn't really welcomed by the family. Do you think the family was a typical one by ignoring the AIDS issue? Do you have any thoughts about their homophobia?

Nancy

TALKING OUR WAY INTO UNDERSTANDING

Some boys develop a deeper, more fully realized understanding of a text when they can share personal meanings and responses with others. Such forums include talking with classmates and the teacher in literature circles, book clubs and reading groups. By going public with their responses, boys increase the connections they can make with those who are reading alongside them, where individual responses are both shared and altered by the contributions of the members, and often by the nurturing support of the teacher.

Literary appreciation can't be demanded, but it can be nurtured and supported. Carl is not a particularly keen reader. He says he remembers when he was trying to learn to read. He would memorize the story and pretend to read, but people inevitably found him out because he would repeat it out of order. One day, he says, he was amazed to find that he was actually reading. How this happened remains a mystery. At school, Carl would rarely bring his own novel to class. If given a free moment, he would play with a tiny skateboard, making it do complicated jumps and turns. But one day he was totally absorbed in *Rule of the Bone*, which had been passed around and enjoyed by Carl's friends. Here was a book that Carl and Nancy, his teacher, could talk about together.

Jay has always read for meaning — omitting, substituting, rephrasing — always struggling to make sense, even when his father would attempt to stifle the guessing, to frighten him into pronouncing word bits, to burden him with too much information. Jay was a risk-taker. Print was always invisible; only the meaning was in sight. When I faltered, he read on. When I panicked, he read secretly. When I chose books unwisely, he read his own selections under the blanket.

D. B.

NANCY: I see you've just finished reading *Rule of the Bone*. You seemed pretty absorbed while you were reading it, and you finished it quite quickly. Why do you suppose that was?

CARL: I liked it. It was about reality stuff. I like books like that. The kid, Chappy—that was his name before he changed it to Bone—real stuff happens to him. It was interesting.

NANCY: What was interesting about it?

CARL: Well, he had a hard life, getting abused by his stepfather and all, and then he runs away, and he and his friend start living with some bikers, and then there's a fire and the main biker guy tries to save him, and the kid gets out but the biker guy dies.

NANCY: So, it was really exciting. Did you like it because it seemed realistic?

CARL: Yeah, but it was far-fetched as well. Like he [the author] made the story more interesting than a real-life story would have been.

NANCY: So you don't think it really could have happened?

CARL: Probably not all the things in the story. He meets this Rasta guy who lives in a bus and the guy starts to take care of him.

NANCY: You mean I-man. What did you think of him?

CARL: At first I liked him. He was really good to Bone, but then it was like he started to use Bone. When Bone got the money to go to Jamaica, then it was like he wasn't interested in Bone anymore. Bone kept asking for advice and he kept saying, "It's up to you."

NANCY: So you thought he should have helped Bone make a decision about going?

CARL: Yeah, I guess, but that's one of the things he (I-man) was teaching: it's up to you.

NANCY: You mean I-man was trying to help Bone realize he had to take charge of his life?

CARL: Yeah, the book was teaching you stuff. It had a moral.

NANCY: But it sounds like you felt I-man should have taken better care of Bone.

CARL: Except it makes sense because I-man was used to not supporting people.

NANCY: So this is what you think he really would have done, but maybe not what he should have done.

CARL: Maybe.

NANCY: Do you think it is the job of adults to help kids?

CARL: Only if they need it; otherwise, leave it alone.

NANCY: What did you think about what happened to I-man? It seemed that he was talking about a peaceful world in Jamaica, one where you could have a perfect life. Do you think that's what Bone believed?

CARL: Yeah, and then this guy comes and kills I-man because of some drug deal, and it's sort of racist too because he says he would've killed Bone except he's white.

NANCY: So I-man didn't have all the answers perhaps? What do you think Bone learned from the experience?

CARL: I don't think he's ever going to depend on anybody again.

NANCY: Really? Why?

CARL: Well, everybody he depended on let him down. His father, his stepfather, I-man . . .

NANCY: Do you think Bone could ever be a good father himself? Could he be different than his father was?

CARL: Yeah, but he might not. He didn't have many good examples.

Retelling a story can help boys to reconstruct the meanings they have made with a text. It allows them to explore the language of literature and reinforces their oral communication skills as they interpret stories and create personal meanings. The urge to share through telling can empower exceptional children to overcome language barriers.

REPRESENTING IDEAS AND FEELINGS VISUALLY

Children of all ages can use art (graphing, painting, and drawing) along with their writing and oral responses to stories. Linking visual with verbal modes of expression can result in better description and detail. There are many ways to see—teachers can capitalize on children's multiple intelligences. Making pictures gives children a sense of freedom of expression because they often feel less restricted by rules and conventions than when they write without pictures.

USING GRAPHIC ORGANIZERS

Boys often choose to display their familiarity with a story through graphic organizers. These include plot relationship charts; story maps, where the main elements of a story are charted to indicate the events that reveal the author's structure; prediction charts; story pyramids; character maps; Venn diagrams; comic strips; murals; friezes; relief maps; story trees; story ladders; and charts showing a sequence of events.

EXPLORING ORAL READING

We may need to re-examine our motives and strategies for including or excluding oral reading in the language programs of our classes. This response mode is perhaps the most sophisticated. Can we give boys the strengths required for oral reading? We want them to approach the process with interest and excitement, accepting the

When Jay was six in grade one, he read everything aloud. He had not yet tuned in to silent reading. On preparing a Christmas tape for friends at the other end of the country, he wanted to read a Frog and Toad story on the tape recorder. After several attempts, he explained to me that it wasn't sounding right, and the two of us decided to talk about the story and attempted to understand the voices. Jay decided that I could read the lines of Toad, along with the dialogue, and he would read Frog's part. Suddenly, the interpretation changed. There was someone to bounce off, to share with, to be stimulated by. The story took life and Jay realized what interpretation was all about. He asked to redo the tape three times, partly for novelty and partly to explore this response to story called oral reading.

D. B.

challenge of bringing someone else's words to life and the risk of discovering a means of communicating ideas.

The benefits of oral reading are numerous. Oral reading can improve comprehension skills, lead to greater understanding of the text, strengthen reading abilities, and enhance interpretation skills. When used as a diagnostic tool with young readers, it allows us to assess pronunciation, fluency, and reading habits.

Oral reading should not be confused with round robin reading, which involves one child reading, then another, and so on. This form of reading is fruitless since it seldom improves reading skills or leads to a deeper understanding/interpretation of print. As well, round robin reading may even decrease a child's understanding and appreciation of the story. A child may decode beautifully, yet understand little.

We can model purposeful oral reading by sharing enjoyable excerpts of a book, by making stories personal for listeners, by reading good stories each day, by reading poetry and plays, and by encouraging children to read only when there is a willing and waiting audience (after an opportunity to rehearse, of course). Teachers can provide a variety of events in the classroom: radio plays, news broadcasts, poetry readings, taped stories, teacher/parent readings, videotapes, and so on.

But I did notice a boy in a red sweat shirt sitting several feet away from everyone else in the room who was giving me more than ordinary attention. After the program was over, he came up and hung around until the other students had left, and then he began to ask me about Gilly. Who was she? Where was she? Then he wanted to know all the other stories—the things that had happened that somehow hadn't gotten into the book. It was one of those times when you know the real question is not being voiced, but I didn't understand what it was. Finally, a teacher persuaded the boy that he must return to class, and besides, she explained, I had to catch a plane shortly. When he had gone, the librarian told me that Eddie was a member of the special reading class who had heard Gilly read. Like Gilly, he was battling his way through a world of trouble. He had never

shown any particular positive interest in books or school until his teacher had read Gilly to the class. And suddenly he had a passion. He was wild about a book—one of those reluctant readers, or even nonreaders, who had to this point seen words, not to mention books, as the deadliest of enemies.

I thought about Eddie for days. Here was a real-live Gilly who not only approved of but actually liked my fictional one. It was better than having a Japanese like The Master Puppeteer. *Well, I decided, I'll just send him a copy. Even if he won't ever read it. At least he will own a book he likes. And that will be one for our side, now won't it?*

Just before Gilly *won the National Book Award, I got a letter from Eddie, and as some of you may remember, I read his letter with, I hasten to assure you, his permission, as part of my acceptance speech. But it feels so good to hear it that I'm going to repeat it.*

Dear Mrs. Paterson,
Thank you for the book "The Great Gilly Hopkins." I love the book. I am on page 16.

Your friend
Always
Eddie Young

From Gates of Excellence
by Katherine Paterson (pp. 14–15)

I admit my mother was a great influence on my literacy development by stimulating my language development during my early childhood. She spent a lot of time reading children's books that held my interest. This experience opened up a new world of imagery for me. She kept encouraging me to read books; however, I didn't push myself to read and I seemed to try to avoid reading. However, instead, my mother gave me picture books with large illustrations. I loved looking at the pictures and visual images. These helped me to understand to which they referred.

I don't think I was really able to read Japanese letters and interpret the meanings during those early years.

My mother created a print-rich environment for me. We had many picture books at home, as well as a wide range of books dealing with Japanese folk tales and Grimm stories.

I also watched cartoons on TV. I used to pretend I was the main character. I used to enjoy re-telling their stories or creating a "make-believe" play. While I pretended, I would fight under the name of justice. This seems to be the emergence and development of my literacy.

Looking back to those days, I found the key to success for learning a second language. My brain absorbed the sentences I heard just as I used to remember the words of songs. When I was given a supporting role in a drama, "Mr. Gumpy's Outing," my classmate, who was supposed to play the main character, was absent on the performance day. The teacher asked me to take his role and I became the main character. I was confident enough to play that role because I had memorized every sentence while listening to the tape many times.

After I was accepted for post-graduate studies at OISE, the course reading in English became the centre of my literacy experience. At the same time, I started to enjoy spending time reading the Japanese newspapers on the Internet. I confess I rarely read The Toronto Star *or* The Globe and Mail. *I still need to use dictionaries to read those newspapers, which makes me want to stay away from them because I feel inhibited. I like to read short articles, but I feel upset when I have to read long ones especially with small print, except for the ones with pictures. I prefer pictures maybe because I had more opportunity to develop my visual literacy with pictures in my early school years.*

Masayuki Hachiya

My nephew Robert, who is a Grade 10 student, whom I would describe as exceptionally intelligent, mature and self-motivated, called me on a Sunday afternoon and asked for help on a comparative essay he was writing on the novels Treasure Island *and* Lord of the Flies. *As I read the draft of the essay, I decided that Robert needed to talk about the book more before he*

wrote a second draft, and I arranged a meeting time.

Five minutes into our discussion, Robert confessed that he had read neither book. He didn't even have the books! I re-read the essay and was shocked at the level of detail and understanding he had demonstrated given that he hadn't read either book. Sheepishly, he showed me the one-line synopsis of Treasure Island *as well as a comic book version of the story that he had dug up from his childhood. A copy of* Lord of the Flies, *he claimed, was in his locker at school.*

I waffled between my teacher outrage and my auntie nurturing roles, but finally asked him why he had gone to all the effort of reading and gathering these other sources instead of reading the books, which, he admitted, sounded interesting. "Too long, no time, other stuff was happening," he offered. Rather than try to find out how this happened to him, I'd like to learn more about the reason for this genuine lack of interest in what I'd consider to be "boy's fiction." I don't believe that it's a question of subject matter, since I am convinced that either film adaptation would have interested him.

Teacher

9. All we do in school is read and write.

Creating a viable literacy structure for boys

Jay needs what all readers need: magazines, books, newspapers, comics, video games, songs and films. And he needs what all writers need: paper, pens and pencils, computers, and reference books. But more than all these, he needs to belong to a community of readers and writers, where his spirit can be nurtured, and his skills can be strengthened.

D. B.

It is important to build a classroom community that has an atmosphere of cooperation and respect for all members. Language arts class offers a context for these sessions, as we need a forum for sharing with the children the many facets of literacy: planning the day's schedule, discussing current issues, reading aloud significant literature, presenting interactive mini-lessons on different aspects of reading and writing, sharing student writing that has been taken to the publishing stage, and listening to talks by guests such as authors.

All the members of the class, including the teacher, are part of the community of readers and writers. This sharing time is an opportunity for everyone to participate in book talk: to offer ideas, connections, and suggestions that contribute to the learning of others. We read independently, but our power as literate humans is acquired from the connections we make to the responses and comments of other members of the community. We want both boys and girls to be significant contributors in our classrooms.

READING TO THE CLASS

As teachers, we can contribute to the sense of community by reading aloud to the class, often, materials they normally would not experience. Chapter books and novels, for example, read a section at a time, can become a high point of the day, a time when children can anticipate gathering together to hear the next installment. When we choose books that support a theme, we can extend children's learning; when we read newspaper and magazine articles, we can model how to find content information and how to stay abreast of current events.

There are many ways in which the reading can take place. We, as teachers, can lead the discussion and model the use of strategies (how to question a text and how to raise discussion issues). Children can read silently. The group can read the book aloud. Children can read the text with a partner. Agreed-upon pages can be read together and others silently. Although class guided reading can be problematic, such sessions can offer unique chances to observe children in a large-group setting—their level of participation, their ability to follow a discussion, their ability to raise relevant issues, and their use of strategies for understanding. As well, you can demonstrate how books work.

Read-aloud time is an opportunity for students to respond through talking together as a community and in small groups. Doing this will help them understand how to think about and to talk about the literature heard or read. I carefully select the text (often a picture book with many-layered meanings). I also like short stories and poems for these events and have found selections in classroom reader anthologies useful. I read the text with as much ability as I can muster, organize the response activities, and conduct a feedback session once the reading and responding are finished.

I structure the response questions the first time, or at least set a context for the discussion, and use the experience as a demonstration of how we work with literature. Sometimes, I have each group discuss a different aspect of the text, creating a real reason for the sharing afterwards. Since students used to ask to see my copy in order to confirm or argue different points, I recommend having some copies of the text available. Working with one group in a fishbowl demonstration can help students see how text conversations work. After the experience, I like to analyze the process with the students so that they can break it down into manageable units that will allow us to discuss their own progress later on.

Having everyone silently read the same novel can also be beneficial if used occasionally and as a demonstration of how literature groups can function. Be sure to select a book that most students can read. Or, offer support to struggling readers, such as having them listen to a recorded version first. This type of activity is a community-building event, where time should be taken to incorporate a variety of response modes into the work.

From **Wordstruck: A Memoir**
by Robert MacNeil

A small boy is being read to. He is warm from a hot bath, wearing striped flannel pajamas and a thick woolen dressing gown with a tasseled cord. He has dropped off his slippers to slide his bare feet between the cushions of the sofa.

It is 1936, a writer's night in Halifax, cold outside. But the boy is cozy, warmed by his mother's voice and imagination.

She read with enthusiasm and delight. If reading the childish stories bored her, she never showed it. She sounded as enthralled, as full of wonder and close-riveted attention as I was. She had a sense of dramatic situation and character and played the parts to the hilt.

PLANNING GUIDED READING

Many boys—and all reluctant readers—can benefit from carefully directed group reading activities, where what they read matters, and how they read is the basis of our teaching. Through guided reading activities, these boys can grow as readers, and feel successful about their literacy abilities.

Guided reading involves grouping children who have similar reading abilities or who need to acquire similar strategies for reading success. Unlike traditional reading groups, where membership is static, guided reading groups re-form constantly throughout the year. The goal of these programs is to have all children read increasingly sophisticated texts—fiction and non-fiction alike—and develop strategies they can use independently. A supportive atmosphere is crucial to guided reading, as is ongoing observation and assessment. Children understand that throughout the day, groups will be dynamic and that they will work in a variety of configurations. Guided reading activities should develop into literature circles and book talk sessions in the years following primary.

The process of building groups that work evolves. A sound knowledge of each child in the class is needed. We must observe and assess children's ability on an ongoing basis, and note the processes and strategies they use to read.

- We can gather together children in flexible groups, whose members share a similar level of reading achievement and use of strategies, and where the children feel comfortable sharing their thoughts and reactions. A maximum of four groups in the classroom is recommended. If there are more groups than this, the process of text selection and working with the groups will become too cumbersome and hard to manage.

- Throughout the day, children will be working within heterogeneous groups. During the year, groups will change continuously. Ongoing observation and assessment of each child helps to determine his or her group placement. Running records, which can be done comfortably with one or two children per group each day, contribute to this assessment.

- Some children may need extra guidance at the beginning of their reading workshop: to understand the reason for approaching the task at hand and to make certain they have the appropriate materials for reading and responding to what they have read. It may be helpful to spend a few minutes with them, repeating the instructions or having them repeat them, perhaps reading the first page together or demonstrating the response activity.

- For many boys and reluctant readers, daily guided reading periods should form the foundation of their reading program. Because these children require the most intensive and explicit teaching, small group instruction using carefully selected texts and directed interaction should result in literacy progress. These students need in-process instruction and assistance as they are reading a selection, to develop strategies that will contribute to their meaning making and allow them to deal with unfamiliar words, structures and ideas in the text.

PARTICIPATING IN LITERATURE GROUPS

In our schedule for literacy growth, we need to create time for boys to work in groups with shared copies of novels that they have chosen from a limited selection of multiple copies. As their ability to follow the routine of participating in literature groups progresses, they may make suggestions as to books that could be added to the resource and may choose to read different books by the same author, or books on a connected theme.

Heterogeneous groups, formed on the basis of students' book choices, permit a useful structure for conducting literature circles with the class. Groups should meet two or three times a week in order to carry on a continuing conversation about their books. They will need to decide on how much should be read before each session, what I call checkpoints, and if they read ahead, group members should reread the portion that will be discussed. The in-depth discussions will be supported by the notes, comments and drawings they have prepared in their reading journals while reading the text.

Participants can share their own personal insights, emotional responses, and connections they are making to the text and to the comments of others. As they begin to hitchhike on each other's comments, they are building background knowledge and incorporating new meanings and different perspectives into their own world pictures. It is important that they speak up and take turns, and refer to the text when making a point. They should be sure that everyone participates, supports each other's comments, moves the discussion along, and helps to keep the talk focused on the ideas generated by the text. Through these conversations, students learn to support their ideas with references in the texts, to pose questions that have real significance, and to accept or at least consider the opinions of others. They will learn about themselves as they deepen and expand their meaning making.

READING INDEPENDENTLY

In independent reading, students select books and read them silently. The difference between this strategy and individualized reading is that while both increase the time students spend reading in school and offer opportunities for learning and practising reading strategies, independent reading provides explicit instruction. It also encourages students to monitor their own reading. The teacher's role is to guide the selection and increase reading. Since many boys find independent reading difficult, we need to set up careful structures or they will read very little.

One means of building energy with reluctant readers in a classroom is to develop an author unit. When boys recognize professional authors as real people, they may begin to see the writing of stories differently. They may come to understand themselves as writers. The personal feelings that children develop from meeting authors promote further reading of selections by those authors, along with books on related themes. Stories are then seen as reflections of those who write them down, and children can see themselves as both readers and writers.

Celebrate authors, storytellers and poets whenever and wherever possible. It is important that as much teaching potential as possible be gleaned from the experience of meeting authors.

In Nancy's Grade 7/8 classroom

Over the course of the year I read my two favorite read-aloud novels: Arizona Kid and The Watsons Go to Birmingham 1963. Arizona Kid is a perfect book for this age. The main character, a sweet down-to-earth 16-year-old boy from a small mid-western town, heads off to visit his uncle in Arizona and work with horses on a race track there. What makes the book special is that in addition to dealing with one of the most fascinating topics for adolescents ("first love") "the first sexual experience" in a delightfully healthy way, it covers a host of other issues and important concerns of this age. Billy's (the kid's) uncle is gay and one of the most charming and lovable fictional characters I've ever met. Billy's relationship with his family is solid and delightful and an interesting contrast to the families of the other kids we meet in the book. Billy falls in love with a gutsy young woman who trains horses, but who suffers from episodes of depression which seem to be related to having been deserted by her mother several years before. The friend he meets at the track is a high school drop-out whose dad is a lawyer, but spends all his spare time preparing for a nuclear holocaust and whose mother seems to deal with life through a cloud of marijuana smoke. The book is very funny because Billy and his uncle have the family sense of humor, but serious issues come up and are dealt with. It is a positive and life-affirming tale. (Those who intend to read it aloud, however, should read it through first to make sure they will be comfortable with the sex scenes. To me they seem to be gently and realistically (tastefully) done, but I am also the health teacher so I am fairly relaxed about discussing this topic with my students.)

The Watsons Go to Birmingham 1963 is also a perfect book for this age. Though told by a bright younger child, it is the story of a family with a rebellious teenager who has his parents at their wit's end with his potentially dangerous behaviors. You grow to love this family, from the totally innocent and loving little sister to the wizened granny in Alabama whom they go to visit. I would gladly have had these parents as my own. All my students recognize the rebellious teen. The fact that the family is African American, however, is not realized by many of the students until we are well into the story, when it becomes clear that racism towards African Americans is one of the themes of the book. The story is about families and love and growing up, but it is also about death and the nature of evil and learning to live in a world in which evil exists.

Both of the aforementioned books could lead to fascinating discussion, but even without any discussion these books are important stories for students to hear.

Nancy Steele

I thoroughly enjoy listening to stories myself and often listen to a book on tape as I drive about the city. I sometimes recommend books I have heard to students I suspect will enjoy them. Often they respond with excitement, talking about books on tape they have listened to on long car journeys. It is rare, however, that I hear tapes that I feel will have the universal appeal necessary for classroom listening. One morning as I listened to W. O. Mitchell reading stories about his childhood, I thought I might have found such a tape. I decided to try it out. A reading is a performance and I suspected it would be much more difficult for a tape player to capture the attention of a class of 30 than a human

reader so I waited until I could play my tape for a small group.

The opportunity arose during an "extended activity week." I was in charge of a group of about nine who had finished all their work. I started by asking if anyone had heard of W. O. Mitchell. No one had. I introduced the author, talking about his age when the tape was made and where he had come from and what was happening in the world during the time he was writing about. I crossed my fingers and pressed Play. At first there was some fidgeting as the group adjusted to his voice and style, but soon I could see that they had become enthralled. I had picked a story about a time in his childhood when he and a small group of friends, while trying to dig a cave, set off explosives and accidentally blew up an outhouse.

Nancy Steele

For my personal enjoyment, I am currently reading Sandra Birdsell's The Russlander. The story is about a Mennonite settlement in Russia in the early 1900s. Being a Mennonite myself, I was intrigued and excited to read a book about my family's history.

The story follows the life of a young Mennonite girl, Katya, whose father works the land of a wealthy Mennonite estate owner. Many Mennonites in Russia prospered, as did a class society within the settlements. The wealthy landowners supported other less-wealthy Mennonites as long as they worked the land. Many of these workers were promised some of the land belonging to the estate owner if they gave several years of labor. For the most part, this never came to fruition. At the bottom of the class society were the Russian peasants who were hired as servants.

My grandparents did not often talk about times in Russia because of the many hardships during and after the Russian Revolution of 1917. During that time, many Mennonites left their homes in Russia, choosing to immigrate to Canada or the United States. Some Mennonites were robbed and killed by bandits who were released from prison during the revolution.

Having not heard many stories about my ancestors in Russia, I must say I am quite shocked by what I am reading. As I read I am in the process of bridging my beliefs about Mennonites in Russia with how Mennonites actually lived and interacted with others. This is the first time where I am struggling with my religious belief system while reading. While reading this text, I find myself meaning-making to such a degree, that I lose my part in the book and have to read it over! It is thrilling to relate my personal stories, my ancestors' stories, Mennonite beliefs, and everything else that shapes who I am to this book. There is constant reference to Mennonite hymns sung in church (many of which we still sing today) and Mennonite foods (which are the absolute best—pastry, meats, bread).

Teacher

I am currently reading seven books simultaneously: my lunchtime book is Tête Blanche *by* Marie-Claire Blais—the English translation, unfortunately—and my bedtime books are: Ionesco's Theatre (can't remember the exact title), Germaine Greer The Complete Woman, *a fiction book based on a true story entitled* J'ai 15 ans et je ne veux pas mourir *(I'm 15 and I don't want to die—the story of a young girl from Budapest in a WW2 concentration camp),* Jean Genet's Our Lady of the Flowers, *more Bukowski poetry and a textbook called* Contemporary Canadian Arts *that is slightly outdated.*

André Tremblay

We mustn't discourage or disparage boys' choices of reading resources. How are you welcoming what boys are reading and opening up options and alternatives for what they might read? Be an enabling adult who helps children to see different, more varied paths in literature than they would find on their own, but respect their small journeys, as well.

Keep a bulletin board of news articles that connect literacy and men: from interviews with authors, to book reviews, to features that highlight the content or issues that are relevant to the books boys are reading. It is vital that we constantly connect print events to boys' lives outside school.

How do you stock books in your school? If there is a school library, do teachers support the librarian by making the collection central to their classroom culture? If you have a bookroom, can you structure a way for accommodating and updating new and reissued titles?

Have you listed the Web sites of authors who talk about boys and reading and who offer suggestions for book choices? Have you organized an author visit to your school or classroom? Do you have a "new book" shelf, where boys can readily see and borrow books? Do you take the time for book talks, exposing boys to new titles and excerpts to promote interest?

In *To Be a Boy, to Be a Reader*, William Brozo summarizes from several research surveys the chief reading interests of boys: humor, horror, adventure/thrillers, information, science fiction, crime/mysteries, monsters/ghosts, sports, war, biography, fantasy, and history. Interest inventories can help us find out what individuals prefer to read, watch and listen to, but they also reveal shared interests of a group, or even of the class. We can use these surveys to develop literacy/literature units and to build resources for group and independent reading. (See "Interview Questions" on pages 115–116. It will help you create your own survey for the boys you are working with.)

In my literacy classes at university, the graduate teachers working with older boys chose two books as their favorites: *Reading Don't Fix No Chevys*, and *I Read It, But I Don't Get It*. Both books talk about real-life boys in trouble with the traditional school literacy programs. They open up options and alternatives for how our classrooms could function if we recognize students' needs and interests and create a curriculum based on our shared findings. The authors talk so honestly and compellingly about literacy in the lives of young men (and women) that I want to begin working immediately using the same honest and forthright approach that these excellent teachers model for us.

C. Assisting Boys in Becoming Writers

10. I don't know what to write about.

Helping boys to develop writing topics that matter

Sept. 8 1988

Dear Dad.

Tomorrow I have gym. Every 2 day I will have gym please help me be dressed properly

Your son,
Jay

As teachers, we sometimes do strange things in the name of literacy. I have saved this letter from Jay—the first one he ever wrote—but in truth, it says little about writing.

D. B.

How do we engage those boys who are reluctant writers in the process of writing? How do we help them choose a topic that interests them, create a first draft without too much pain, consider how they might revise their work, and then edit it for sharing with others? We are faced with the same questions year after year. Hughes Mearns, in *Creative Youth*, wrote about these issues in 1930, and we are still struggling. Our chief goal remains to motivate boys into using words and images to represent their thoughts and feelings so that two things happen:

1. With their words in front of them, they come to see what they are thinking. Until they freeze their thoughts on a page, they can't examine and reflect on where they are in their world picture.

2. They have a chance to see how others view their work, so that the meanings they began with can grow and clarify.

We can't gloss over the fact that writing is hard work, and revision and editing even harder. But we can help boys choose issues that matter and find for them reasons for having their works read and considered by others. The following questions can be used to assess our practice.

• Can we accept the topics many boys want to write about—humor, wild adventures, word play—and work with the young writers on aspects of form and style? If we can, these boys will lose some resistance to writing and begin to look forward to sharing their revised pieces of writing with others.

• Have reluctant writers had opportunities to read selections by others their own age, friends or past students, so that they have models in mind for what they might develop? No one can create in a vacuum; everyone needs a map of the terrain if they are to get anywhere.

- Do we have all sorts of "mentor" writings for them—strong novels, poems, picture books, non-fiction, articles, and comics—so that they can find frames and borrow structures for their own ideas? If they are writing a script, have they read any to see how this genre works? How many types of poems have they seen before trying to harness their own efforts?

- Do we plan for guided writing instruction where we work with a group of boys on writing techniques and strategies, such as conventions, genre study or technological help? Groups can form and re-form as students change activities and need explicit instruction.

There are several things we can do to make writing easier for some boys. We can record a boy's dictated story on the chalkboard or on chart paper, acting as a scribe, and then provide the boy with a copy of the story for rereading, so that he will see his ideas and words in print. We can ensure that boys have access to a range of writing materials and tools, including special notepads, clipboards, graph paper, poster board, stationery, pens, markers, pencils, and especially, computers. We can compose a piece of writing with students, clarifying aloud how we work as writers, what we need to revise and how we can strengthen our work. We can offer extra needed help as boys proofread their own writing, letting them read their work aloud to themselves and note incongruencies, and use computer spell checks and other reference resources.

We need to let more boys in on the secrets of writing.

WRITING IN NOTEBOOKS

Ralph Fletcher says we need a place to record "our thoughts, feelings, sensations, and opinions or they will pass through us like the air we breathe." Writing notebooks can become a surprisingly valuable resource for boys. Boys can capture the seeds of ideas that can be developed later as independent writing projects. They can jot down images or events, note memorable words or phrases, record snippets of conversation or a line from an advertisement, recognize an example of rich language use, or sketch artifacts that may be significant, and glue poems and documents that hold further interest.

We can open up the possibilities of the records, feelings and observations that can be kept in a notebook through mini-lessons. These might range in focus from retelling family stories to creating a web of ideas about an interesting issue, from providing a prompt such as "I dream about . . ." to asking students to remember characters and incidents in books they have read.

CREATING A FIRST DRAFT

Many boys need help to generate ideas. It is equally important that they have an opportunity to discuss their ideas with one another.

When he was eight, Jay announced that he would be keeping a journal, and that it was to remain private: "I'll be leaving it on the counter each day, Dad, but you are not to read it." And I haven't (yet).

D. B.

During a brainstorming session, they can write down all of their ideas so they have something concrete to work from. Some will select writings from their notebooks to use as inspiration for a longer piece. Some will begin to compose during this stage of the writing process, determining which ideas should be developed further. The main purpose at the drafting stage is to set down their thoughts and feelings. Until they have written what they want to say, exactly as they wish to say it, children do not place much emphasis on editorial issues.

Bear three things in mind.

- Some writing does not need to be revised. A list of things to do doesn't need revision; a letter to a friend or relative sometimes does. A project for sharing *always* requires editing.

- Never expect a first draft to be perfect. Most professional authors revise their writing several times before they are satisfied with their work.

- Students should keep all their drafts. Doing so will help them to see their progress as writers.

From On Writing: A Memoir of the Craft
by Stephen King

If you want to be a writer, you must do two things above all others: read a lot and write a lot. There's no way around these two things that I'm aware of, no shortcut.

I'm a slow reader, but I usually get through seventy or eighty books a year, mostly fiction. I don't read in order to study the craft; I read because I like to read. It's what I do at night, kicked back in my blue chair. Similarly, I don't read fiction to study the art of fiction, but simply because I like stories. Yet there is a learning process going on. Every book you pick up has its own lesson or lessons, and quite often the bad books have more to teach than the good ones.

FINDING PATTERNS FOR WRITING

A mentor text is an example of writing in the mode that the student has chosen. For example, a boy opting to write factual reports might be directed to feature articles clipped from newspapers or magazines. Students interested in writing poetry should be directed to a variety of poems and poetic forms, especially non-rhyming types of poetry. A student who wishes to write a picture book must investigate a variety of picture books. Other writers might want to look at editorials, letters to the editor, plays, and diaries. The teacher can provide mini-lessons that demonstrate the various genres available to the writer. Well-chosen picture books, poems, and feature articles can be presented through book talks and read-alouds and will help children see the many shapes that their writing can take.

When I was travelling on a speaking engagement in another city, I opened my suitcase and found a Smarties box with a note wrapped around it.

Dear Dad,

A treat for you!
Hurry home.

Love
Jay

Real writing from a real writer

D. B.

When I was 12, I took up "pigeon breeding" as a hobby.

I was a very naive boy in every way upon becoming a pigeon breeder. The birds and the bees, however, were right in your face when pigeons mated. It amazed me that the bizarre balancing act which had to occur, amidst all those feathers and claws, could actually result in anything! But results were frequent, in the form of two or three little eggs, guarded very assertively by the mother.

I never knew that the instinct to protect one's young was so strong until I walked out to my roost one morning to check on two young females, one with three newborn squabs, and the other who had just recently brooded and laid three eggs. I knew something was very wrong right in the pit of my stomach the instant I neared the gate. Every pigeon in the roost was on the far right side of the roost, out in the open, clinging desperately to the highest little octagon of chicken wire that they could find to keep away from the ground. I counted quickly and could tell that two pigeons were missing. Something had very recently happened, or had been so traumatic to the birds in the roost that they were in a sort of stupor. I opened up the gate and saw two heads on the ground. I instantly knew which birds they were—the mothers. I know that our memories play funny tricks on us as the years pass, but I am almost certain that there was only one body, laying on the ground nearby. I distinctly remember looking down at the body and seeing one of those hard-as-rock pea seeds in the bird's gullet. I felt sick to the stomach, then panicked, as I realized that the mothers were not in their nests any more. Reluctantly, I looked into the nest which had been home to the newborn squabs. All three were lying stretched out, their huge distended bellies beneath them, prickly little baby feathers all over their little pink bodies, closed black orbs for eyes which had never yet opened to see their mother. I swore and swore in the way that only a twelve-year-old can. I decided in my wisdom that it was a snake (I had and still do have a horrible phobia of snakes, and wasn't thinking logically enough to reason out how a snake could rip the head off a pigeon!) or a cat or a raccoon. I was most disturbed that only one body was there. Where had the other one been taken? Had the animal got full and left it behind, or did it get scared away? Worst thought of all, would I find a skull-less skeleton one day in the tall weeds surrounding the pigeon roost? My anger that a mother bird could be killed, and thus result in several other deaths, stayed with me for a long time. It was, to me, as a 12-year-old child, totally unfair. I pictured them both sitting fearfully, yet with instinctual determination as they sensed the movement close by that signalled danger. I remember wanting to kill whatever it was that killed the mothers instead of one of the other pigeons. I felt hatred and it was more powerful than I wanted to know I was capable of. I tried to hatch the eggs by wrapping them in a towel and resting them atop and finding them browned on one side, burnt no doubt by the 100 watt light. I buried them under a beautiful burgundy Japanese maple tree, in our front yard pet cemetery (several cats, two budgies and numerous goldfish had all been ceremoniously interred there over the years by my younger sister and I, two professed Unitarians who couldn't quite shake God and Heaven from our belief system), next to the headless mother and her three squabs, who had all been wrapped in Kleenex and sealed inside a Hush Puppies shoe box.

Michael Ross

That year my brother David jumped ahead to the fourth grade and I was pulled out of school entirely. I had missed too much of the first grade, my mother and the school agreed; I could start fresh in the fall of the year, if my health was good.

Most of the year I spend either in bed or housebound. I read my way through approximately six tons of comic books, progressed to Tom Swift and Dave Dawson (a heroic World War II pilot whose various planes were always "prop-clawing for altitude"), then moved on to Jack London's bloodcurdling animal tales. At some point I began to write my own stories. Imitation preceded creation; I would copy Combat Casey comics word for word in my Blue Horse tablet, sometimes adding my own descriptions where they seemed appropriate.

From On Writing:
A Memoir of the Craft
by Stephen King

Some part of me always thought that my female students were more at risk (than male students) in every area. It seemed to make sense in my head; after all, most positions of privilege and authority in our society are held by men, and so therefore, one thinks that those must be fairly literate men. But a closer examination would probably show that those positions are not always held by the most literate. Sometimes, we have enough skills and knowledge to do our job, but those skills don't always transfer to what we do at home, if we don't have writing lives outside of our workplace.

Looking back, I think that a higher proportion of girls wrote on their own time, for the love of it. But I think that I only realized that, this year, when a big chunk of the class male population started writing "for fun."

Elementary teacher

11. Guess what happened to me?

Helping boys to share and shape stories from their lives

We need to promote the recalling, sharing and shaping of boys' life stories as useful resources for reading and writing. The stories that students tell about themselves should be honored in our classrooms. Through their stories they build their self-esteem and sense of belonging in the world, and, of course, they come to understand how stories work.

> *During those years, Jay brought in the mail; and sorted it into two piles—his and mine. All the junk letters are his, along with the Nintendo newsletter, the* Junior National Geographic *and each week, a letter from Uncle Bill, with a note and a riddle included. Such care our friend Bill takes for my little boy, building a relationship and developing Jay's literacy skills. Reading and writing have to appear as normal, every day functions if children are to join the literacy club. I want reading and writing to envelop Jay's life, not as drill or homework or punishment, but as a means of experiencing the intensity of life itself. Children can write down what has happened to them, and they can read about other people's lives in order to make sense of their own. We can help them to begin to notice the richness in their own lives and the wonder and power of print. Stories, words and images in their own writing can be drawn from their own family anecdotes, from the happenings of the day, from their memories of classroom activities, from recess, from after-four play, from songs on tapes and games on video.*
>
> *D. B.*

Children are in a privileged position as they develop into story-tellers and storymakers, not fitting easily into stages or ages. They work with stories in order to understand the process of building life narratives, telling their tales out loud to find out what they have said and how they could say it more effectively.

As storying teachers, we can find ways to both inspire and enable our children

- to call upon their memories of life experiences as starting points for building stories;
- to turn their stories into tales worth telling to others;
- to make others' stories into their own, not through memorization, but through reworking, retelling and reliving them until they are deeply embedded in their story chests;
- to be guided and inspired by other memorable story experiences told by significant tellers;

- to seek opportunities for listening to and telling carefully crafted personal life tales in natural and authentic ways, investing each story with meaning and art;
- to gain insight into their own stories through the process of sharing in the story circle, deepening their own storytelling practice and transforming themselves from within the tales they tell of their lives thus far;
- to be strengthened by the storying process so that competence, confidence and self-esteem will accrue and be part of other public speaking activities.

Here is an example of a boy drawing on a life story for writing.

In Search of the Perfect Running Shoes
(I dedicate this book to my brother because he loves to wear expensive running shoes, and to all people who would wish to have high quality running shoes.)

I had enough of wet socks, smelly feet and worn out running shoes. I had to throw away the "High Flyers" my parents bought for me over a year ago!

I desperately needed a new pair of running shoes. However, instead of a cheap pair of sneakers, I would purchase the best running shoes on the market.

I realized that such running shoes would be quite expensive. Money would not stop me, for I had saved up all my paper route pay for the last seven months.

I started my search by making a list of some of the shoe stores that sold high quality running shoes. My list included: 1. Collegiate Sports at Islington Avenue and the Queensway 2. Kinney 3. Champs 4. Footlocker, all the last three stores at Sherway Gardens.

After school on Friday evening, my dad drove me to Collegiate Sports. In the store I found all sorts of running shoes for many different kinds of sports, such as soccer, basketball, tennis, football and baseball. I looked around for about half an hour but I did not find anything I wanted to buy. Since it was getting late, my dad decided to return home but promised to continue the search for my running shoes the next day.

By 9:00 on Saturday morning, we were on our way to Sherway Gardens. The first shoe store we visited was Kinney. I looked closely at many different brands of running shoes displayed in the store.

There were L.A.Gear, Nike Air, Adidas Torsion, Brooks Hydroflow and Reebok E.R.S. I spent half an hour trying on different styles, but I did not like any of them.

We continued walking in the plaza until we came to "Champs Athletic World." As soon as we entered, I spotted a whole rack of Reebok Pumps E.R.S. I hurried to the rack and started looking for size 6. I found all sizes except my size. I was so disappointed. I asked the manager whether he had Reebok Pumps in size 6 in stock. When he replied he did not, I walked out of the store feeling frustrated.

So my dad and I walked until we arrived at "Footlocker." We went in and looked for Reebok Pumps. When I found them, I searched for size 6. As soon as I picked up the Reebok Pumps in my size, I shouted, "Alright! At last!" I tried them on and they fitted perfectly.

These Reebok Pumps were the best style and quality running shoes I could buy. The price of the Pumps was expensive but with the paper route money I had saved, I could afford to buy the best running shoes available.

Now that my search for the perfect running shoes was over, I felt like the happiest boy in the world because I owned the most perfect running shoes in the whole wide world.

All About the Author

Hi! My name is Michael. (I am ten years old. My hobby is collecting basketball cards.) I am in grade 4 class. If you really like running shoes you should read my book. Enjoy it!

I have no memories of my parents reading to me. I have no recollection of books being displayed in our household, and I don't remember any occasions of going to a store to buy books of my own. It was the Wychwood and Dufferin libraries that offered me the books of my youth. My house was located half way between the two buildings, and I would visit each library on alternate Saturdays. I was drawn to biographies and autobiographies and would choose a book because of the brightness and newness of the cover. The orange-bound copy of The Life of Alexander Graham Bell *stands out. My first memory of reading fiction was* Homer Price *by Robert McCloskey. I loved the story about the rich lady who lost her bracelet in a batch of doughnut batter. I love the story, and I love (to this day) the illustration of the piles and piles of doughnuts.*

I chose to read books that I thought were humorous and continued to do so until I moved to a new house, and a new middle school, and a new library—the Bookmobile—that visited the local shopping plaza every Thursday. I usually chose popular fiction to read and was challenged to read a new novel each week before the Bookmobile returned. When it was time to go to high school, my reading was restricted to the titles we were "forced" to read in our English classes—Eagle of the Ninth, The Pearl, Wuthering Heights, The Scarlet Letter. *It wasn't until I was past my university days that I returned to self-selecting books and became immersed in the reading of fiction. Philip Roth was a favorite author.*

These days I am interested in finding new titles listed in the New York Times *and visit bookstores two or three times a week. I currently have piles of books on my bedside table and I can't wait to read some new purchases of titles by Rohinton Mistry, John Irving and David Sadaris—and a biography (of Pauline Kael)—to read on an airplane, in a park, or in the comfort and calm of my bedroom.*

Larry Swartz

When my son Jake was in third grade, the one required summer reading book for his whole class was Little House on the Prairie. *Jake's first impression? "Why are we reading this? Reading is for girls." Jake is now in high school, but along the way he has worked* through required readings of E. B. White's Charlotte's Web, *Alice Walker's* The Color Purple, *Michael Dorris's* Yellow Raft in Blue Water *and Toni Morrison's* Sula. *Jake's current impression? "Reading is definitely for girls."*

I grew up with five brothers (no sisters). Everything was a guy activity in our house—eating, wrestling, cooking, reading, more eating and wrestling. I remember hearing my mother read Dr. Seuss aloud to us and being absolutely amazed. I wanted to read those words myself. I never thought of reading as something for girls.

We always had books around the house. And there were, of course, fewer entertainments competing with reading when I was growing up. Undistracted by cable TV, the Internet, DVDs and Playstation 2, I could be bored enough to be driven to discover on the summer cottage bookshelves copies of Tales of Edgar Allan Poe, *Reader's Digest's "I Am Joe's Liver" and Boccaccio's* Decameron. *I read to make my own discoveries. The more I read, the more I wanted to read.*

Today, I'm the father of a girl and a boy. My daughter, Casey, is as much a reader as Jake is not. As a baby, she read books aloud in her own made-up language. Growing up, she devoured entire shelves of *Nancy Drew*, the *Babysitter's Club*, *American Girl* and *Sweet Valley High* books—for fun. Jake has never been one to pick up a book for fun. His classic answer to my question "What books are you packing for vacation?" is still "Why would I take books? This is supposed to be a vacation."

I know some of this is just who they are. Not every child is a reader. But I worry that more girls than boys are readers because we're not showing boys that reading is as much a guy activity as a girl activity.

Jon Scieszka

On the home front my son and his father engage in a constant battle over maintaining a daily journal. B-O-R-I-N-G! Knowing that he is a socially interactive individual who enjoys using the Internet, I decided that writing to him via e-mail would be a more effective strategy in motivating him to write while having him naturally observe what good writers do. In my exchange, I am sure to include a balance of information and some thought-provoking questions to assist him in forming a response. Our dialogue so far has centred on films that we have seen together and ideas that arise in David Booth's class.

Elementary teacher

12. Can I be in the play?

Drama as a source for reading and writing

We need to develop drama units in which boys can express and reflect upon their ideas and feelings artistically, cooperatively and safely. Outlining the practices of another teacher, Nancy Steele, is probably the best way to show the potential of scripting as a way to promote reading and writing.

In Nancy's writing program in Grades 7 and 8, each student creates a 20-minute, one-act play. The students know that about 12 of the 60 or so plays that will be written will be performed and that every student in the school will appear in one of those performances. Nancy, who has been doing this for many years, has a collection of videotapes of plays written and performed in previous years. She sometimes shows them to students once they have begun to write. Very few of her Grade 7 students have written a play before, and their experience with a script is mostly from television. Since stage plays have their own rules and difficulties, she tries to take them slowly through the process of planning their plays.

First, Nancy reads two or three excellent short plays that appeal to this age group. Two are taken from a collection of plays written by high school students. One, *Hey, Little Walter*, is about a poor family living in a ghetto whose son becomes involved in drug trafficking. The playwright has written notes at the end of the play about how she came to write this particular play. She says that although she wrote the play in her senior year, the character of Little Walter began to live in her head when she was a sophomore. That's because many of her friends were being drawn into the world of drugs and many were dying. The play is about the people and problems that the playwright experienced. Nancy explains to her students that they will probably write better plays if their characters are composites of people they know.

The students' first task is to figure out who their play will be about and what problem that person will have. They talk about the plots of plays they have seen on TV sitcoms or in the movies, and they identify the problems in each. Some students find it fascinating to realize that there is a careful structure to most of the drama that they see every day: a problem is introduced early on in the story which reaches a high point of tension close to the end and then is resolved. They begin to list the types of problems they've seen playwrights use on television and in film. Eventually, they realize that there are a limited number of problems and that they can categorize most into about ten types. The class then talks about problems with which they may have had some experience (bullying, jealousy, family members who have become sick, parents who worry too much, peer pressure, and so on). Nancy explains that they will probably write a better play if, like the author of *Hey, Little Walter*, they choose a topic they feel strongly about.

Finally the plays are written and, with the help of readers, about 12 are chosen to be performed. Everyone is encouraged to read for as many plays as possible. The playwrights draw up a list of actors they would like and casting takes place one day after school. The playwrights sit in a circle, each getting one choice at a time. They go round until all plays are cast and everyone has a part. The next day the casting is posted and although a bit of conflict resolution is required, there is surprisingly little weeping, wailing or gnashing of teeth.

The plays cover a wide variety of issues. I have seen the productions for more than four years and have enjoyed them immensely. The energy, the camaraderie, the commitment to all aspects make this project a shining example of student work. To see all of the boys working alongside all of the girls to bring these plays to life honors what strength our students possess.

Here is an excerpt from one boy's script, a satirical look at an unpopular politician.

A Day in the Life
Play—Scene one

(Setting: School stairwell/hall way/classroom)
10-second pause
(Tumbleweed ball rolls through from stage left to stage right, sfx: desert wind accompaniment)
10-second pause
sfx: school bell ringing
(Kids 1, 2 and 3 walk on stage right, Kid 4 and Cedric enter stage L.)
sfx: background noise
(Cedric sits down at base of stairs, kids 1 and 2 enter classroom, kids 3 and 4 exits stage R.)

Cedric: (rummaging through backpack) (angrily) Dangit! I could have sworn I had it! (Throws backpack angrily to floor) Dangit! I had that letter!

Leith: (Enters stage L/holding piece of paper) Hey, Cedric, you dropped this! (Sits down beside Cedric, gives him paper, leans back)

Cedric: Yo, thanks, Leith! I've been lookin' all over for this! (Puts paper on top of backpack)

(Mr. Henderson enters stage R. rushes into classroom, acts as if teaching i.e. draws pi on blackboard, etc.)

10-second pause

Leith: (gestures with hand towards note on top of backpack) What does that mean . . . politician?

Cedric: Didn't you hear? A politician fell out of a plane on the weekend—been running around inside the school ever since. The principal called to get rid of it but no one called back.

Leith: (blinks sarcastically) A . . . politician . . . fell from the . . . sky?

Cedric: Mmhmm. That's what this is. Written consent from the government and zoo that if someone comes to claim him they can get him back—without this, they can't! It also says that if no one comes to claim him, I get to keep him!

Leith: Let me guess: you've always wanted a pet politician?

Cedric: Yep. Since the weekend! I don't want anything to happen to Mikey!

Leith: Mikey?

Cedric: The politician.

Leith: Oka-aay whatever. (Looks at watch) Oh, jeez! I'm late for class! (Leith exits at run stage R.)

Cedric: (grabs knapsack, forgets note on staircase, exits at run stage R.)

(Janitor walks on stage L, carrying pole-spike and garbage-holder-on-stick.)

(Janitor stops, looks perplexed, goes over to staircase, stabs paper with pole-spike, puts it in garbage-holder-on-stick, exits stage L.)

Cedric: (enters stage R. at run, yanks open classroom door, barges in, stumbles, reaches out for support, grabs Mr. Henderson, both lose balance and fall behind teacher's desk. Only Mr. Henderson's feet are visible.)

Mr. Henderson: (exasperated, but voice remains calm in a strained way) Cedric Freeman-Wilson, how many times have you been warned not to come to class late?

Mr. Fogelman scanned the few lines, and glared at me, face flaming in anger. "This isn't what I assigned!"

I should say that I had nothing against Mr. Fogelman at that moment. He was okay—the kind of young teacher who tries to be "one of the guys," but everything he does only shows how out of it he is. I just wanted to set the record straight.

"Yes, it is," I told him. "The assignment sheet said to give our honest opinion, write what was our favorite part and character, and make a recommendation. It's all there."

"Old Shep, My Pal is a timeless classic!" roared the teacher. "It won the Gunhold Award! It was my favorite book growing up.

Everybody loves it." He turned to the rest of the class. "Right?"

The reaction was a murmur of mixed reviews.

"It was okay, I guess."

"Not too bad."

"Why did it have to be so sad?"

"Exactly!" Fogelman pounced on the comment. "IT was sad. What a heartbreaking surprise ending!"

"I wasn't surprised," I said. "I knew Old Shep was going to die before I started page one."

"Don't be ridiculous," the teacher snapped. "How?"

I shrugged. "Because the dog always dies. Go to the library and pick out a book with an award sticker and a dog on the cover. Trust me, that dog is going down."

"Not true!" stormed Mr. Fogelman.

"Well," I challenged, "what happened to Old Yeller?"

"Oh, all right," the teacher admitted. "So Old Yeller died."

"What about Sounder?" piped up Joey Quick.

"And Bristle Face," added Mike "Feather" Wrigley, one of my football teammates.

"Don't forget Where the Red Fern Grows," I put in. "The double whammy—two dogs die in that one."

"You've made your point," growled Mr. Fogelman. "And now I'm going to make mine. I expect a proper review. And you're going to give it to me—during detention!"

From No More Dead Dogs
by Gordon Korman

I remember hating the Poetry unit. I remember enjoying reading others' poems but I knew, inevitably, the culminating task would be to write my own poem(s). I knew I wasn't very good at it and that I found it very hard. I don't remember using any models or playing with poems—like using an author's structure and changing the words. It was just like: see how you heard all of these wonderful poems by professional authors—now sit down, be quiet and write your own!

One very positive experience stands out in my mind: Canadian Literature with Mr. Bland (ironically, this WAS his name!). I don't remember everything that we did in his class, but I do remember that it was often exciting and fun. He was doing "stuff" that other teachers weren't. This class was where I got my first A in my new school (this was good since I wasn't doing particularly well that year). One very interesting activity was writing a radio play about "Captain West," a made-up character, with two other girls. We often worked with others, we explored a variety of genres and we did "neat" things with the interesting literature we read.

Elementary teacher

As the autumn leaves changed colour and began to fall, Todd still read outside during recess. He always sat cross-legged on the same bench. The students called it "Todd's bench". During my yard duty rounds, I often observed the intense expression on Todd's face, as he turned the pages of his book. I thought about one of the parents in my class who announced that she hoped her son would develop a "joy for reading" this year. "I want my son to read like Todd," were her exact words.

Todd's love for reading did not prevent him from interacting with his classmates or having friends. Friends were very important to Todd and he was always very loyal to them. Luckily, Todd's friends understood and respected his ardent desire to turn the pages of his book, instead of tossing a ball at recess. When the days began to grow colder, a few of the children in the class expressed their concern over how Todd was going to read outside when it snowed.

"Let's build him a fishing hut!" suggested one child.

"You mean a warming hut," corrected another student.

"We can build it around his bench," added another child.

"It will need a special heater and light," said one of Todd's best friends.

"We can even get him one of those special suits that people wear when they go to the North Pole," explained another classmate.

The students quickly began to draw detailed diagrams of possible "warming huts" for Todd, so that he could continue reading outside at recess during the winter months.

Although Todd was thoroughly amused at the thought of his very own "warming hut", he decided he would be warmer and more comfortable inside.

Dalia Besasparis

13. Do poems always have to rhyme?

Revealing and understanding emotions through poetry

September 13

I don't want to
Because boys
Don't write poetry:

Girls do.

And so begins Sharon Creech's novel *Love That Dog*, the story of Jack, a student in Room 105—Miss Stretchberry's class—who resists his teacher's poetry lessons as strongly as possible. Finally through her skills and patience, Miss Stretchberry helps Jack understand what this art form holds for those who need its gentle power. The author of the book cleverly has her character write about another real writer as part of his classroom project—Walter Dean Myers—and it is this interaction between the two that moves Jack into a more meaningful literacy life.

From **Knots in My Yo-yo String**
by Jerry Spinelli

In sixth grade our teacher assigned us a project: Make a scrapbook of Mexico. I found pictures of Mexico in National Geographic and other magazines and pasted them in my scrapbook, for which my father made a professional-looking cover at the print shop. Then I did something extra. It wasn't part of the assignment. I just did it.

I wrote a poem.

Three stanzas about Mexico, ending with a touristy come-on: "Now, isn't that where you'd like to be?" I wrote it in pencil, longhand, my best penmanship, on a piece of lined classroom paper. I pasted it neatly on the last page of my scrapbook and turned in the project.

Several days later my mother walked the three blocks to my school. She met with my teacher, who told her she did not believe that my poem about Mexico was my own work. She thought I copied it from a book. (Hah! If she only knew how few books I read, and never one with poetry!) I was suspected of plagiarism.

I don't know what my mother said to her, but by the time she walked out I was in the clear, legally at least. Five years passed before I wrote another poem.

Anyone who has worked with adolescent boys is aware of the unique subculture many of them inhabit, at least some of the time. In this subculture, being seen by other boys to be "masculine" is tremendously important. This concern can lead many boys to adopt stereotypical masculine behaviors, such as risk taking and rule breaking, and it makes the stereotypical "feminine" behaviors and attributes, such as sensitivity and expression of feelings, anathema. If they do talk about their feelings (other than outrage), it is generally to a girl and almost never when other boys are about. The boys who are most successful in this culture are often seen by the others to be the "cool" or popular group; those not accepted by the group often identify themselves in relation to that group as "the brainers," "the weirdos," the "arty" types or varying combinations of the three. In these other groups, emotional sensitivity usually doesn't receive much play.

So when one of Nancy Steele's "cool" Grade 8 boys asks, "When are we starting poetry?" or when she overhears one boy say to another in the hall, "Oh great, it's poetry today," she gets a thrill.

Nancy teaches writing in single-sex classes, and poetry is either the second or third writing unit each year. Clearing her table at the front of the room of student-written stories, she stacks books of student-written poems which, like the storybooks, have been published in the classroom each year for as long as she has taught writing. On the day they begin the poetry unit, she makes sure everyone has one or two of the little classroom publications and everyone is asked to look for a poem to share. The poems, like the poets, are in turn racy, rude, tender and funny. They range emotionally from ecstasy to despair. There is something there for everyone.

The boys want to know about the poets. Some recognize older friends; some find poems about themselves written by older siblings. "He wrote that? I didn't know he could write!" "That is *so* Jeff . . ." The lives of the people they know are there for them to admire: poems about fishing, skate boarding, skiing, love; poems about what it is like to be 13 and too short, too lazy, too uncool. Everyone finds a favorite and reads it out. They want to know the stories behind the poems. "How come this one is anonymous?" "Why did you let him use *a swear word* and you told me to take it out of my story?"

"Read the poem," Nancy answers. "Can you see why he needs it? You have to save the strong language for when you really need it."

Sometimes, Nancy hears the Grade 7 students grumble about how the poems are too good, that *they* could never write poems like these. She carefully explains, "Every student has at least two poems in each book each year, so yes, somehow everyone does write two wonderful poems. But these poems are not first drafts, nor do they come out of nowhere. I will give you specific instructions that will help you find the words you want."

What often surprises Nancy is that boys who have shown no particular affinity for story writing become prolific poets. It's as if freed from having to write complete and sequential sentences, they allow themselves to play with words, images and emotions. Often, their most poignant poems are very short, just a phrase that expresses a thought or a worry. Given the dignity of the poetic form, these thoughts arrest us as readers, and we celebrate these young minds as they fool with different structures and patterns for holding emotion and thought, using rhyme when it works, pauses when required, repetition when appropriate. In the sections below, you will see young male adolescents shining from their time with Nancy.

Night Soccer

The soft glow of the street
  lights
colours the newly formed
  dew.
Like many little crystals.
My foot
Speckled by wet grass

directs the ball towards the
  net.

The cold smell of grass
drifts upwards into the humid
  night.
The cool creek bubbles
and I look at my watch
2:36 a.m.
not yet,
I'll sleep later.

Untitled

I'd love to be new born—
to explore my life
with no weight on my back or
  my heart.
Oh, how I wish I had a fresh
  start.

Growing Minds

I've **R**ead so many books
I've been **E**nveloped in
  amazing stories
of **A**dventure, romance or
  mystery all in one
I was **D**ead to the world but
  learning at the same time
Inspired to have adventures
  or solve mysteries
New or old it doesn't matter,
  read them all
Growing minds

Peace

Warm breeze on my face
Wind whispers quietly and
I sit in the sun

Bed

Lying in soft security
surrounded by a blue wisp of
cloud warm and happy. Red
numbers are a damning glow
that sentences me to yet
another day of waking
trauma. They read:
8:30

Storm

I sit on a sofa listening to the
soft falling tears of a sky
wracked with clouds. They fall
uninterrupted until a boom of
warming signaling the Earth to
beware the fury of Zeus'
blade knifing to the ground in
angry light, flickering and
cracking a reminder to
humans, that you do not
control all.

My Life is like a Tsunami

My life is like a tsunami. It
  picks me up.
Swirling, bubbling around me.
  Faster and faster.
Collecting momentum as it
  rushes forward.
Getting bigger and more
  powerful,
Only to smash me to pieces on
  some town.
Then it all starts over.

Finally, the poem below, a moving, dreamlike piece written by a boy of seven, captures what we hope all boys will one day achieve —power with words and the things that really matter in their lives. Somehow, child poems seem to hold the most hope.

a poem

a poem is not alwes esye
as your pensl glids aloug your paper
But
if you wate fof it to come
you can creat your own
werld. and the penny in your
pigy bank can tern into a poem
that may be big as a Lion
or as small as a mouse.
Your loose tooth will fall aut
into a dreme, that leads toward
the Light.

Kiernan, age 7

ACKNOWLEDGING CONTEMPORARY MUSIC

Some contemporary music has poetic quality and can be used as a springboard for exploring poems. One young male teacher in my graduate education class chose as his final project to chronicle a unit with his Grade 10 class on contemporary music lyrics. He had the students, working in groups, select six of their favorite songs and compare them with poems from several anthologies he had collected. Each group presented the songs in sound and on overhead transparencies, and the unit was extremely successful, for both the students and the teacher.

However, some members of the graduate class were shocked when they read and heard the lyrics. They accused the teacher of inappropriate professional behavior, ignoring that he felt he had worked hard with the boys to select the least controversial lyrics that they could live with.

How on earth will we help such boys to see options and alternatives in their literacy lives if we refuse to recognize their preferences? We need not appreciate, but we shouldn't disparage.

William Pollack suggests using these discussion questions after listening with boys to their music selections:

- *What are they singing about in this song?*
- *What does it mean?*
- *Who do you think mostly likes this music?*
- *What do you think they like about it?*
- *Do you agree with what it's saying in its lyrics? Why or why not?*
- *Is there anything that disturbs you about this song? If so, what?*
- *Can you think of any people who would find this song disturbing? Why?*
- *Do you think this song accurately reflects the way things are in real life?*

I am a poet, and reading work that I find exciting transports me to a mental realm where anything seems possible. Mundane concerns are transcended as my consciousness expands just enough to take in the text's novel configurations and ideas.

I like to read experimental writings because they push the boundaries of language—and language, as Terence McKenna observed, is what the world is made of. We create reality (both internal and, to a great extent, external) by thinking it into being. André Breton, who founded the Surrealist movement, declared that "the imaginary is what tends to become real." Reading works of the imagination can trigger visions and intuitions capable of inspiring new worlds: cognitive worlds, cultural worlds, even concrete worlds. When an author defies the limitations of tradition, she takes a step into linguistic terrain which may lead to revelation. I like to take part in that adventure, and all I need to do is read her words. Maybe they'll work for me or maybe they won't, but it's always worth the bother because when they do work, there's an almost delirium-inducing charge, a neural exhilaration that causes me to look at my existence in a new way.

Besides all that, reading can be a blast. The brilliant words of another can deliver me to states of hilarity, awe, terror, languor, illumination and an expansive range of other inner conditions. When your mind resonates with a writer's words, your thoughts, perceptions and dreams can be dynamically altered. It is for that sometimes sublime alteration that I read.

Steve Venright, poet

My first poetry writing exercise is a trip into a memory. Everyone closes their eyes and I talk them into their past. I do many variations on this exercise. Here is one: Go back to a time, let it be summer, when you were very happy. It can be in the recent or not so recent past, but you need to remember it. It can't be a story you were told. How old are you? Remember how it felt to be that old. Now put yourself in the memory. Look around. What do you see? Are you indoors or out? Look up. Notice the sky or ceiling, whatever is above you. Now look out at eye level. Now look at the ground. Notice all the little details.

Take a minute now to open your eyes and write down what you could see. Let's go back to the memory. Are people there with you? Animals? Look for colors. What is moving? What is still? Add these to your notes. Go back into your memory, but this time open your ears. What noises are there? the wind? machines? voices? birds? water sounds? Write them down. We go like this through the senses: touch—the feel of your clothes on your body, the sand on your feet; taste—the salty sweat, the cold, sweet, drippy popsicle; smell—the pine trees, the chlorine of the pool. Make notes.

My last instruction is to remember how you feel. Is it a single feeling or a jumble of emotions? What are they? Write them down. I tell them that if they have done the exercise, then everything they need for the poem is there. All they have to do is tell the story with as few words as possible. They don't need complete sentences, but they want to listen for the rhythm of the words.

Some boys will have written a page of notes, some only a word or two. It doesn't matter. All those who have participated in the remembering will be able to do it again another time, perhaps to remember a less pleasant time but one they need to explore. If there is time, they work on the poem in class. If not, at home. I try to make sure there is time for everyone who wants to share a little something: what they were remembering or a phrase they liked. It's a nice thing to do together and generally we leave feeling happy and hopeful about these potential poems.

Nancy Steele

14. Does spelling count?

Helping boys in building word muscles

"I am a Bear of Very Little Brain,
and long words bother me."

Winnie-the-Pooh
by A. A. Milne

My exact feelings, especially when I am writing long words down and having difficulty with their spelling. Like Pooh Bear, I need help with those special words that wiggle and waver in the heat of writing. I have learned to leave their print representation for the moment and to go on putting down my ideas, returning later to worry over them and to seek help from friends and other print resources. But for many people, especially boys, spelling is such a great problem that they avoid writing, use simple words, take far too long pondering, or give up caring in frustration.

Part of the problem is that spelling is usually viewed as a black and white issue. For ten years, I have typed book lists for my students in Children's Literature. One of the annotations concerns a novel titled *Dorp Dead*, by Julia Cunningham. Five typists have corrected that title to read "Drop Dead." Each time I asked to have it changed, the typist challenged first my spelling and then the author's use of the misspelling. "A bad model for children," I was told. I think I prefer Winnie-the-Pooh's attitude to spelling, expressed in A. A. Milne's *Pooh's Alphabet Book*: "My spelling is Wobbly. It's good spelling but it Wobbles, and the letters get in the wrong places."

Boys who are reluctant readers and writers need to build an ever-increasing word bank of immediately recognizable words, effective ways to discover unknown words in their reading texts, and useful strategies for spelling words in their writing. They can notice how letters fit together, the patterns involved in word construction, the ways we can take words apart to discover their inner workings. In working with them, we must remember that word power is cumulative and lifelong, and aim for significant individual growth from year to year.

Word walls with different categories, sorting and categorizing words, word searches, word puzzles, silly poems full of word play, cloze exercises, magnetic letters and word board games all help students to notice how words work. Becoming an effective speller is a gradual process, and we may need to explicitly direct children to focus on a few words at a time, words connected by structure or pattern, so that word knowledge can be incremental. In our classrooms, some students will be working with dozens of unrelated words, but boys in difficulty will need our help in taking a few words apart and putting them back together. We need to focus on one word that leads to three or four more. Classifying a boy's errors in a piece of writing may help him to understand a particular spelling pattern.

Beyond seeing how words work, students, I hope, will become wordsmiths, noticing significant and special words, recognizing when words are used effectively or in interesting ways, marking words that sound delightful or funny, and noting words with unusual spellings. Recommended Books for Boys offers some good wordplay book titles on pages 122–123.

Playful approaches and games may be our strongest allies. Computer programs are beginning to offer intriguing ways for building word strength with spelling and vocabulary games and puzzles. They also offer support for struggling handwriters and spellers. Many of the games on screen offer openings to limited readers for taking part in print-based activities, with less frustration and defeat than in much paper-and-pencil work.

Sometimes, we are told to use a published spelling program. If so, we can choose those activities that focus on patterns and word building. Doing this will ensure that the students' time is spent as meaningfully as possible. Most of my errors are typos, created by my inadequate keyboarding skills. Spell check brings up Canadian/U.S. spelling differences, but misses homonyms.

Proficient spellers have a high degree of competency in frequently used words and use multiple resources for the challenges that occur in writing. Similarly, we can teach our students to use a variety of strategies when checking the questionable spelling of a word. (I am pleased to see a student circling a word in a rough draft; it shows the speller knows what he doesn't know.) Students who check spellings are raising their spelling consciousness.

My nephew, Max, age 10, is at Camp Manitou. I received his camptionary postcard. All he had to do was check off the appropriate boxes that reflected his message on the postcard (oh yes, his grandmother had printed my address on the card prior to his leaving for camp, so he didn't even have to write my name and address) e.g., I am having fun, please write back, my cabin is great, etc. Very efficient for him. And no sweat involved! However, he did add his own three words: I love you. That was it. He didn't sign his name, but I knew it was his handwriting (age, gender appropriate and level for cursive writing). That's a boy for you!

Then my niece, Bess, aged 12, writes me a letter in return for one I had written her (she's at the same camp) on her own stationery, about 150 words, chatty, with humor, a P.S., an envelope properly addressed!

So, what's my point? It's not the age difference . . . at all. It's the intrinsic gender stuff—a boy avoids the chat, the words, the details, someone else does it for him!

Sandy Katz

At the age of 15 my younger brother dropped out of school. John was a learning disabled student with technical aptitude. In the world of cars, he experienced success. He had an innate ability to diagnose the most challenging

technical difficulties in cars. To be able to diagnose these problems, he was required to follow technical manuals as complex as Gray's anatomy. Yet at school, John was a failure because he could not perform school literacy tasks. John successfully completed his apprenticeship program in auto mechanics. For more than 20 years he worked at several General Motors dealerships and was promoted to shop foreman. Four years ago he decided to enter the Faculty of Education to complete a diploma in Transportation Technology.

Currently, he works as a supply teacher, as secondary school reform has eroded the number of positions in his field. As he reflects on his life, he is reminded of the importance of reading. As a frustrated adolescent he was convinced that reading had no real relevance in his future. Throughout his apprenticeship, he came to realize that being able to read very complex automotive manuals was the key to "fixing those Chevys"! His passion for reading pervades all aspects of his life and stems from his feeling of competence and control.

I see him supporting his learning disabled son and empathizing with the challenges his child faces daily. Cameron does not possess his father's technical aptitude for cars; he prefers the computer. As I observe this father and son and their literacy practices, I am reminded that the issue of boys and literacy is of paramount importance.

English consultant

I spoke very candidly with Mike and asked him what his goals were for our time together. He replied that he was willing to do anything to learn to read better. He said that he wanted me to help him, as I had already assisted him with some of his math difficulties.

Mike was part of the lowest reading group in his classroom. His teacher expected each group to read aloud at least once per week and answer a list of questions from the back of each story. I suggested that Mike read the required story ahead of time so he could practise before he had to read in front of the class. This strategy began to pay off and was evident in his growing confidence, and smoothness of reading during these stressful times.

Student teacher

If boys need help and motivation in planning, revising and editing their written work, then why can't we employ text types other than personal narrative for boys and girls to explore, opening up their familiarity with the whole world of written forms?

What connection can you make in your classroom between writing and the subjects you teach? What if the children saw science and social studies as opportunities for drafting their knowledge and questions about the issues you are exploring? Are there opportunities for reports to be written by a group whose members will share their research with the class? Are there directions and instructions children could write for their classmates to follow in conducting an experiment or designing a machine? Could a book report be seen as an opportunity to persuade others to read it? Can history offer opportunities for retelling, for creating maps of journeys taken, for explaining why particular events occurred? Could children derive respect as writers from their peers as they work with forms and formats often ignored in writing time?

Do you have plenty of mentor texts, or examples of specific genres, for children to explore before they write? (Some could be student work from previous years.) I remember Joby, a Grade 3 student, writing a report on Chilean refugees that her group had interviewed. Group members drew up their questions, conducted interviews, summarized their findings, and shared their reports. I have kept Joby's work for 20 years to remind me of the power that can be found in much of non-fiction writing.

You may find it helpful to read Tony Stead's *Is That a Fact?* Stead offers dozens of suggestions for working in non-fiction modes with young children. The teachers I work with also appreciate Randy Bomer's *Time for Meaning*, where he describes activities for older students, working with each genre inside powerful and extended units.

Are *you* connecting what boys write and talk about with what they are reading, so that *they* begin to connect the different literacies in their lives?

Would it help you to teach poetry the way Nancy Steele does: in single-sex groupings? Nancy finds that the boys move into sensitive issues more quickly and more deeply. They share their writings in mixed collections and enjoy reading the thoughts of others.

Boys often say that they don't know how to improve their writing, that teachers' editorial comments are too general. But inside the books by Ralph Fletcher and JoAnn Portalupi are strategies for focusing on one particular element of writing at a time. Be sure to look at both *Craft Lessons* and *Nonfiction Craft Lessons*. If you select one item for a reluctant writer to work on each time he revises his work, there is hope that he will alter how he writes in the future.

Patsy Porter's doctoral thesis observed that when boys work collaboratively with computers on projects, the work becomes more sophisticated and complex. We traditionally think of computer work as solitary, but her report suggests that we incorporate pairs and small groups into our technological writing. How would this work in your school? Are there computer lab times that could assist you?

How do boys and girls feel about computers and information technology in their school and academic lives? Do girls feel under supported? What types of activities benefit the students most? How many students have access to home computers? How can your school redress an unfair situation with respect to home availability?

Many educational systems are leveling the books so that a child's growth as a reader matches a chosen text. How can we ensure that those children at the beginning stages of reading also meet and enjoy powerful stories and poems? Through read-alouds, shared reading, or literature circles, could we draw individual boys into more complex texts?

D. Structuring Literacy Events for Boys

15. Can you show me how to do it?

Modeling and demonstrating literacy strategies

When we demonstrate our own thinking "out loud," we make our thinking visible to our students, so that they see how we handle a piece of text before, during and after we read. When students can see our own processes in action, they may be able to use these strategies in their own work. It is helpful to choose a text that is easily accessed, so that students can focus on their reading strategies.

All of us learn from the demonstrations of others. For example, we learned how to ride a bicycle by watching others ride. We may have learned to use a computer by following the demonstrations of a proficient user. We will continue to learn from the demonstrations of others throughout our lives. Demonstrations give us concrete examples of a concept we need to learn, a strategy we need to practise, or knowledge we need to acquire.

Demonstrations can happen at any time during the school day. They are conscious, explicit attempts to show children how something is done. They can be spontaneous (e.g., the outcome of a conference with a child) or planned (e.g., when we see a child struggle with a concept that can be made more explicit). They can be in a range of situations: on an individual basis, with a small group, or with the class. They can have a powerful and lasting effect on the learner. Classrooms need to be filled with relevant and functional literacy demonstrations.

Select a short text that will enable you to say aloud what you are thinking as you read it through. You might begin with a passage that you have thought through first, or use a sight piece that will give the students an authentic picture of how readers read. You can share the text on an overhead transparency or give the students a copy for them to follow along. Choose a selection that will focus on a particular strategy that you feel the students need.

CONDUCTING MINI-LESSONS

A mini-lesson is a brief, focused lesson that allows us to demonstrate or teach a specific skill or idea in a short, purposeful way. Reading, writing, or thinking strategies can all be demonstrated using mini-lessons, which are often generated by the needs of the children. As well, mini-lessons can be used to review classroom procedures, to show ways to think about what one has read, and to teach specific reading skills.

Introduce the concept of mini-lessons early in the year by letting the children know the behavior expected of them (e.g., where do they meet for mini-lessons?). Keep in mind that content mini-lessons are most effective when delivered to small groups of children or a single child. For mini-lessons dealing with topics that children will refer to repeatedly (e.g., punctuation), teach the mini-lesson using chart paper. When completed, the paper can be hung together with related charts and displayed on the wall for children's reference.

On a more subtle level, remember that you are a significant member of the classroom literacy community. You can share samples of your own writing, books you are reading, newspaper columns that upset you with their gender stereotypes, cartoons on the overhead projector that make you laugh, poems that make you sad with remembrance, forms you are filling out, such as surveys, junk mail you have received as samples of specific genres, film reviews you agree or don't agree with, recipes cooked the night before, CDs you enjoy playing, e-mails other students have sent you.

PROMOTING BUDDIES

Reading buddies can play a significant role in building boy readers.

I remember in the 1970s the city of Hamilton, Ontario, had 200 senior citizens reading to children throughout the school system. These volunteers, trained and supported with a good book collection, went out into the schools where they simply read aloud—one on one. Where are these programs today? At least now students in senior grades read aloud to older people in residences as part of their community service. Could organizations such as Big Brothers give a book (from lawn sales or remainder shelves) to those they mentor? Let's make literacy intergenerational.

What buddy programs could you begin in your school or community to promote reading? Who learns more—the young child seeing an older boy reading with him, or the Grade 8 boy sensing the satisfaction that comes from the delight and the learning in the eyes of the primary child? Why is such a program not mandatory for all senior students? And what about having reading buddies by e-mail, where boys can keep in touch with young men studying to be teachers or with university students in social work? You can begin to brainstorm a buddy list for the boys in your life, many of whom would be bookless and hopeless without such a program.

I spent a lot of time as an adolescent in the library, but again I do not remember many of the books. I know I liked non-fiction, for example, war stories including books on both war strategy and front line sagas. I also read encyclopedias. We had two or three sets in the house and I would take two or three volumes to bed for bedtime reading. I liked reading about the world. Also National Geographic for the same reason. Also these were the years I discovered Mad magazine. I loved this magazine for its spoofs on all things held sacred in society (e.g., family, movies, work, etc.). The humor and satire was usually right on the mark and, as the magazine did not accept advertising, not much was missed or off limits. It was subtle humor, you had to look for it, not gross like Frank . . .

I like books that explain, describe or at least explore the subtleties of the world, especially as new experiments and information suggest our most recent basis of understanding matter are demolished beyond recognition. Human behavior fascinates me, and if behavior is a response to the information collected by the physical senses, then I need to understand how we collect and process information—brain chemistry leaps to mind. Is it mind over matter, mind working with matter?

For me, none of this is academic. If we do not find our place in the world—and that is both a physical and more importantly a spiritual issue—we will destroy the earth's ability to sustain ourselves. The speed of destruction will preclude our species' ability to evolve to a new physical order. For me, pollution on all scales is a psychological process first, and it is at that level we need to engage the issues. That is why I read what I read today.

I am a newspaper junkie. I read everything I can get my hands on. I subscribe to one newspaper; the rest I will read if I can do so for free. I realize all newspapers in Toronto share the same news sources so I know they will all contain the same news (only the presentation of the news is different). I am not reading the newspaper for news as much as I read it as "ritual." I read over breakfast and lunch and am quite unhappy if it is not delivered in time for breakfast. At other times of the day, I read it to break the day's activities up—I finish one activity, but before beginning the next, take a tea and paper break—it is a way of putting structure in my very unstructured and haphazard day. Reading a book couldn't do the same job, simply because a book is too long. Newspaper articles are just right, anything and everything from 10 seconds in length to 10 minutes. I have always read newspapers, at least since my early teens; at this point it is ritual.

At the library, while waiting for the rest of the family to get material, I will read any magazine I find on the shelf, even if it is a topic I know little about. Again, I have a short period of time (up to 30 minutes) and magazine articles are the right length. I will read professional magazines for the classifieds—that is one way to find out about really neat, out-of-the-way stuff.

Male of 49, with a focus on environmental studies and urban planning

I was not an avid reader when younger, but enjoyed reading some books. At age 16, I had a pivotal experience in high school which changed my view of reading: I was to prepare for an oral examination which counted 40 percent of my final mark on the book Zen and the Art of Motorcycle Maintenance. I was very tense coming into the exam room. However, my teacher told me to relax and pull up a chair for my feet and just take a seat on one of the desks (informal) like, and talk about my favorite parts of the book, some of the events etc. Although I could not remember many character names, I was able to talk about events and even relate some of them to personal experience.

I received the highest mark on the oral exam and I began to see myself more as a reader and I have enjoyed reading ever since.

Grade 5 teacher

16. How can I find out?

Recognizing inquiry as a central motivation for reading and writing

Inquiries and investigations can grow from a topic or an issue drawn from the boys' own interests or questions generated by a curriculum area that cause them to want to find answers or solutions. This kind of writing can grow from science or social studies as well as from novels and picture books, and these inquiries can last for a few days, or several weeks. Some aspects may be included as homework, but the classroom is the best place for identifying a topic, formulating questions, and developing a plan of research. Intensive long-term research projects immerse the students in authentic reading and writing experiences. Our role is to help maintain their interests and sustain their efforts by creating carefully structured goals and schedules so they know what to do at each stage of the project.

LETTING INTERESTS DRIVE RESEARCH INQUIRIES

Structuring units of work around critical questions that are generated by the students provides a framework in which "to teach strategies, concepts, and textural knowledge that we have privileged as a profession" (Smith and Wilhelm, p. 189). The energy that boys will expend on classroom projects in which they have ownership grows exponentially as they work on what they find useful and important, on what matters to them. Sustained engagement involves a deep exploration of ideas, capitalizing on the expertise of the students themselves, as they construct their own learning. It is often difficult to bring these embedded inquiries to a close. These boys are caught up in their own efforts to share their learning, driven by the "imperative of the quest."

Government directives dating from the 1920s and 1930s suggest that we incorporate these enterprises into our planning, but timetabling is often the enemy of extended learning. How can your school encourage a deepening and broadening of issues arising from the literature and the information that students meet in your initial lessons? How can you expand the potential of the resource you begin with, so that students move into the response with the energies from their lives "outside school"?

HELPING BOYS ORGANIZE INFORMATION

Boys often need help in planning how to structure the information they have found through their research inquiry. We can help them with ways to sort, select and arrange their data through mini-lessons that demonstrate the use of categories or sections with titles and subtitles as guides for formatting. Examples and student samples often give boys frames for organizing their own investigations. Rather than demanding effective outlines for writing projects, we need to offer guidance and models for building effective structures. In the end, we want to be able to see what they have learned through their intensive research writing.

Boys can gain help from sharing their initial questions with a partner or a small study group, breaking the topic into bite-sized chunks, helping with categories and headings, suggesting other resources, offering support with the presentation of the information—how to inform others with text and graphics, how to connect the different sections to create an overview.

Boys and, of course, girls can collect information for inquiries in a variety of ways:

- Searching the Internet and Web sites can provide a rich data bank for locating information. However, the material is often unreferenced and some sites are unsuitable. With guidance, though, the electronic search can open up worlds of knowledge to young researchers.

- Appropriate software, CD-ROMs, videotapes and films can give students access to information, often in a dramatic documentary form. A group of students can preview several videotapes on a monitor set up in the hallway.

- Students can conduct interviews which, when recorded and then summarized or transcribed, offer primary source data to support an inquiry. Besides in-person interviews, students can conduct conversations on the phone, by e-mail or on a chat line on the computer.

- First-hand research sites can include another classroom; libraries; a field trip location, such as a museum or science centre; government buildings; a theatre group; or a shopping mall.

- Students will have real reasons for using references such as encyclopedia, all types of dictionaries, *Guinness World Records*, maps and atlases, telephone directories, or statistics to support and substantiate their investigations.

- Research inquiries can lead to a variety of other print resources: magazine and newspaper articles, manuals and guides, brochures, catalogues and programs of events.

- Documents offer special insights for research: letters and diaries, wills, archival photos, vintage books, land deeds, surveys, reproduced or downloaded from the Internet.

Presenting their inquiries allows boys to practise oral communication and make written and visual demonstrations of their research. I am impressed how overhead transparencies cause students to carefully consider how they will represent their findings. In some schools, students can move into PowerPoint presentations using the computer set-up. Displays and bulletin boards let other students benefit from the research, and young investigators may want to have a guide sheet for observers to note their learning and to record further questions.

The students in a secondary classroom created a class magazine about their common interests. The boys chose cars.

IMPORT SOCIETY

Can anyone tell me the feeling you get when an older RX-7 flies by you and your Civic that you invested nearly $30,000 into and the RX-7 is completely stock besides a set of rims?

"JEALOUSY" is what goes through my mind, pure jealousy.

This 1988 Mazda RX-7 was bought by Al Ratford brand new and was used for basic purposes until one day when a young kid with an Eagle Talon Tsi pulled up next to Al at a red light. The Talon took off at the first sight of the green light and as a joke Al wanted to see what his turbo RX-7 could do. So Al slammed the accelerator to the mat and within seconds was flying past not only the Talon but everything around him. Since then Al has added 17" Blitz rims wrapped in Falken rubbers.

This 3.0 Litre turbo RX-7 has since dusted 5.0 Litre Mustangs, Camaros, Supras, and yes, even those pesky little Civic pocket rockets, and doing so without throwing a penny into the motor. But as Al gets older and older, the longer the old RX-7 stays in the garage.

Justin
Editor, Import Society

LOCAL CIVIC WINS BEST OF SHOW

This 1993 yellow hatchback surprisingly will be travelling home which is just down the road with the "best of show" award from the Toronto Car Show.

This little yellow Civic brought home the "best of show," "best paint," and "cleanest conversion" (due to his '95 si engine swap). Paul intends to add a Greddy stage 3 turbo, Greddy intercooler, and Greddy blow off valve.

Maybe then Paul will claim all the awards at the local car show.

Adam
Editor, Import Society

LETTER TO THE EDITOR

Dear Import Society,
I read the article regarding the Accord with hydro's last month and was shockingly surprised and very impressed. I normally stay away from hydraulics but this Accord was really irregular. I myself have an Accord (same body style) and couldn't decide on what kind of drop I wanted on my car, but thanks to your article, I have now made up my mind.

If you guys could recommend any good shops that do hydraulic installations, it would greatly be appreciated.

Thanks for submitting my response.

Sincerely,
Joe Brown, NY

"SPECTACULAR" . . . the only word good enough to describe this immaculate '98 Civic. Sean (21) who lives in Los Angeles, California, took up an interest in customizing imports when his older sister's boyfriend took Paul for a ride in his 1992 Civic hatchback that was tuned to run low 10 seconds in the 1/4 mile, way back when Paul was only 13 years old.

Paul's first car was a 1993 Del Sol with 17" ADR rims, Weapon R intake, and Koni adjustable coilovers.

Not long after Paul got it, it was stolen. Which brings us to the present and the 1998 Honda Civic Weapon R loaded Si.

This beautifully loaded Civic comes with more Weapon R upgrades than the speed shop that sells it.

The paint job alone is a show stopper on this car, but when Paul steps into it, this Civic screams. With a Weapon R intake, exhaust, valve cover kit, and fuel pressure regulator not to mention the Jackson Racing supercharger, this is one car you don't want to mess with. Thanks for the interview, Paul.

Justin
Import Society

FEATURE ARTICLE

We are reaching 2002 and cars are reaching new technological advances and they are grabbing the eyes of many. Also the cars of the new millennium are now showing the more youthful look instead of the class of dull-bodies sedan. Cars are becoming more compact and are coming with many more gadgets in them. One of the newer looks would be the BMW 7 series. With 333 horsepower, 4.4 liter and a sleek body, the BMW has come into its own. But prices will not change unfortunately. For 7 series BMW you would be paying close to 60,000 dollars. But if you have that kind of money to spend, then this is the car for you. Also on the market is the new Mercedes Benz C230 Sports Coupe. Mercedes is now going for the hatchback look. Unfortunately, not my kind of look. But this Mercedes is

trying to reach the younger buyers to [t]he best of their ability by now throwing in a bit more horse, smaller body and a premium sound system. It also is a 2.4-liter which will be a welcoming change for once. For all this you would be paying a surprising 27 thousand. Not bad from the number one car company. Also some new practical cars to come on the market in 2002 are the Subaru Impreza WRX, the Cadillac CTS, the Audi S6 Avant and the much awaited Acura RSX Type-S. These are just a few of the many cars coming our way in 2002 that will grab the attention of many.

LETTER TO THE EDITOR
Hi! I'm Zach and I am a car owner. This is just my opinion, but I think that the cars of 2000 and beyond

are becoming too weird for me. I mean the shapes of some of the models that are coming out are just too wild. I mean, it seemed like just a year ago that cars looked practical, but now they are coming out with these new futuristic cars that wouldn't appeal to any age bracket. I think they should just stay with the models they have been creating. They were doing just fine. Also, they are making cars today much faster and if this is the case, then why do they keep the speeding limit so low everywhere? It's a shame how the cars of the new millennium are turning out.

Zach

---

17. How am I doing? What do I do next?

Demystifying assessment and evaluation processes

When we discuss assessment, we talk about the ongoing observation of children, including anecdotal observations, conferences, reading profiles and checklists, and portfolios. Outcomes of assessment procedures allow us to plan programs for children that reflect their current learning and capitalize on their strengths to develop other areas of growth. Evaluation refers to the judgments we make on the bases of our assessment practices. Assessment, then, informs our daily teaching, and evaluation—marks and grades—is used when communicating with parents and other educators.

The essay that follows was a response to a poem I had written years ago; it was later used on a literacy assessment exam. A teacher thought I might enjoy reading one student's response to my ideas and mailed me a copy. I am always impressed with students who can make meaning without discussion or feedback in a testing situation.

Here We Go Lobster Loo

I went to a very expensive restaurant
With my mother
And my grandfather
In Halifax.
She said to have lobster—
Melt in the mouth lobster.
But she didn't tell me
Lobsters alive,
All red and crawling
In an old aquarium.
I chose the saddest one.
They boiled him alive.
Alive.
I listened to my plate.
No sound.
Then I took the pliers
And cracked and crushed
And scraped the pink flesh
Into my red mouth.
I told her I loved lobster.

But they belong in Nova Scotia
With my grandfather,
Not on my fork.

D. B.

Here we go Lobster Loo

I chose to write about this poem because it reminds me of myself when my father brought Lobster home to be prepared for dinner. I did not know Lobsters were to be alive before cooking. Looking at those poor innocent creative being prepared to go into the pot of boiling death water made me cry because they were alive when father brought them home, but with no sound or movement on my plate.

The part of the poem which mentions "The expensive restaurant" did the same to me as it did to the Boy because I had to eat it, very upsetting to me but I had to eat it. Many of my family members did. I did not want to see my father upset because of the tremendous effort needed to catch these creature and for me not to eat them would break my father's heart.

To devour them like them like that made me cry not physically, but mentally. For, in my mind I also heard screaming. Horrifying screams coming from my lobster as I cracked him, crushed him, scraped flesh from his broken body and eat that flesh from the creature screaming, the screaming only heard by my ears.

In my mouth, the flesh from the creature tore at my glands, my taste buds and at my mind. The taste of this creature made me feel like spitting out, but the thoughts of my father's work catching the creatures made me eat.

I chew because there are many lobsters in the sea which I can make happy by letting them live among themselves but one father to make happy, by being his wonderful son.

The quality of our evaluation reflects our assessment procedures. We need to assess all areas of a boy's growth in literacy: to look at the books he reads, the amount read, the degree of pleasure derived from reading, the strategies used, the quality of the responses, the ability to reflect on the learning, the awareness of reading process elements, and the ability to self-assess personal reading growth.

You can share with the children your assessment goals and the role they play in shaping their reading program. Boys need to track their learning, books they have read, reflections on reading, response methods they have used, areas in which they are confident and skills they would like to improve; collect pieces they have published; and organize peer and self-assessments.

HELPING BOYS PREPARE FOR TESTS

Tests, formal and informal, are helpful when they assess learning that is measurable and when they reflect the content of the program. However, in reading, many components cannot be isolated. Interpretation of reading tests must be handled carefully.

There are a number of reasons a child may not perform well on an isolated test, ranging from a bad night's rest to a problem at home. You and your students should view the test results as a way to check the effectiveness of the program. In this way, children will feel less anxious and not be concerned that a poor test result will influence their learning for the rest of the year.

In considering lower than expected results in some class-wide testing, we should also keep in mind that a variety of factors may influence reading results. One obvious example is a class where the majority of the students speaks English as a second language. Variables must be taken into account when discussing such results.

Some boys do not achieve well on standardized tests that require inferences and personal responses. Practice sessions with similar items and lots of discussion can help these boys to learn how to handle those types of activities, and at the same time, increase their understanding of how to read.

Practice sessions using the types of texts and questions boys will meet on upcoming tests are most useful. If we organize these sessions carefully and connect them to the regular classroom work, we can help boys to work within the confines of the formal test situation.

Frequently I enjoyed the pleasure of praising the success of students at the Hockey Training Institute Private School. Almost invariably my joy was tempered by comments such as, "Yeah, but, your school is special education with a modified (read "simplified") program."

This virtually undisputed opinion assumes that any student who finally succeeds in a different program is too academically incompetent or psychologically impaired to achieve at the "normal" academic level. In other words, the problem can only be due to student deficit (at either end of the competence spectrum: too bright or too slow). The labels are always attached to the student, proving to all that the individual is not capable of regular learning in the regular system.

In fact, the assumption of student deficit is so pervasive that even apparently loving and supportive parents respond with disbelief and accusations of school incompetence when a previously "poor" student starts to succeed academically. One such incident occurred where the student was a classic "D" producer all through elementary school and into high

school. After 18 months in the private school, however, Brad was consistently and comfortably working at a B+ level. When the final report card arrived home, Brad's father called complaining that his boy was incapable of achieving the recorded results, concluding that the school must have an inferior program.

A school can be too successful if virtually no one believes its practices and evaluations are valid vis à vis the regular system. In fact, Brad's apparently startling performance resulted from a number of realities, none of which had to do with inferior programs.

It is the attitude of everyone in this school: administrators, teachers, support staff, parents and most importantly, the students. Everyone believes all students are capable of succeeding academically. For some students it takes more work and time than for others, but none are physically, mentally or emotionally incapable of academic success.

Even hockey players and hyperactive and bored students can learn to read . . . and write and draw conclusions from historical data and solve scientific

equations . . . If teachers know what students can do, they will teach their students what they can learn next.

"It's what you feel about what you do that counts," was stated many years ago, but it is as true today as it was then. It applies to each student and equally importantly, to each student's teacher.

> Diva Anderson,
> Hockey Training Institute Private School

I began tutoring my 12-year-old nephew Cameron who is in Grade 7. My nephew was diagnosed with Attention Deficit Hyperactive Disorder, Oppositional Defiance Disorder, a General Anxiety Disorder and a learning disability at the end of Grade 2. He has been receiving academic support in language and mathematics on a withdrawal basis for one hour per day.

When I interviewed Cameron about his attitude towards reading and his reading preferences, he stated quite emphatically that the reading specialist did not teach him to read during the summer tutoring sessions. He firmly believes that the technical manuals for each of his video or computer games, such as Red Alert, made him into the reader he is today. Cameron explained, "I liked reading the manuals because they had the keys or codes that I needed to reach the next level of challenge in the game. Sometimes my friends download cheat sheets from the Internet. I memorize the codes. I can even spell words like 'oblivion' and 'annihilation' and I know what they mean. I feel smart playing these games. I don't even realize that I miss lunch or dinner because I am so into it. Anyway, riding the subway was really boring. Reading my manuals made the time pass quickly. Everybody on the subway was reading something!"

Today Cameron prides himself on being an avid reader. He lulls himself to sleep after making a selection from his night table which is littered with a stack of computer manuals, a current issue of his favorite comic book, the Guinness Book of Records and several non-fiction texts on astronomy, insects or military life. He has just finished reading Holes. When he emerged from his room, he said: "I know how Zero feels." He began reciting passages from the text and related many details about the insufferable Texas sun, the threat of the scorpion and Stanley's overly superstitious nature. He is now reading Star Girl as his fascination with girls and Arizona saguaro cacti cannot be contained!

Cameron is a highly literate student, but his teachers are not aware of how he practises literacy out of school. In the interviews I conducted with Cameron, he expressed feelings of inadequacy when he was at school. He mentioned being bullied by his peers because of his placement in a learning disabilities class. Cameron's literate behavior is untapped and unrecognized in his school setting.

English consultant

William Brozo, in *To Be a Boy, to Be a Reader*, offers us a valuable construct for helping teens find entry points into literature, and by doing so, expanding their literacy competence. He has developed a curriculum model based on traditional and positive male archetypes: Pilgrim, Patriarch, King, Warrior, Magician, Wildman, Healer, Prophet, Trickster and Lover. He uses these archetypes as a way of tapping into the imaginations of adolescent boys. As boys engage with literature that explores the unforgettable and self-affirming experiences that connect them to the lives in these books, they alter their own stereotypical notions of what it means to be masculine. In doing so, the boys have a chance to move into the academic possibilities that reading brings, an acceptable and worthwhile male experience. Can you build literacy/literature units in similar fashion, using the suggestions in his bibliography?

We have to find ways to help a difficult boy move towards literacy. We know that if one person connects with him in a caring way, his behavior can change in quick order. But in crowded classrooms with several boys like him, the chances of connecting are fewer. Two brief stories demonstrate the power of positive intervention:

> One child in a school hallway told another, "In there, that's the Reading Recovery room. I can't read out here. But in there, she helps, and it's a miracle, but I can read." Another child asked the Reading Recovery teacher if she could help his brother learn to read. "You helped me and he's worse. Could you help him?"

If a boy feels powerless and confused, and acts these feelings out by being defiant and difficult at school, how can we respond so that he will want to change? How can we coach him towards new behaviors? Are there outside clubs, sports organizations or volunteer groups that the boy could be referred to? Can we break the behavioral problems into understandable bits? For example, could he put his head on his desk for two minutes until he calms down? Could he write down his feelings, or suggest an alternative to the way the difficulty is being handled? If confrontation doesn't work in our lives as adults, can we find different means of guiding a child at risk?

If boys most frequently choose non-fiction books to read, and if girls need to be encouraged to read print genres other than fictional

narratives, why do we seldom include these types of texts in our classroom writing programs? If boys do better on literacy tests that incorporate non-fiction forms, and if girls do less well with these types of texts, should we not begin to incorporate these forms into our classroom programs?

How can your school structure opportunities for single-sex groups of students? If students are taught by a team of four or five teachers, perhaps you can flex the timetable so that groups of boys and girls can meet. What observations do the teachers and the students make from these sessions? Are there any differences in the learning behaviors or learning outcomes of the separated groups?

Kathleen Gallagher, in *Drama Education in the Lives of Girls: Imagining Possibilities*, chronicles her drama teaching in an all-girls school. She offers us strategies for freeing and strengthening young voices through role work and reflections. We quickly see the value of some single-sex classes at this age and stage of development.

How can you "activate" your classroom so that boys (and girls) who have trouble sitting still for long periods have physical activity throughout the day? Can they move to a work centre after listening as a class? Can you plan a physical game after each subject time, just to let their bodies move? Does your school value recess activity and ensure that the boys who need it most do not lose it as a punishment? Can you incorporate different groupings as often as possible so that boys can move to a new location with new team members?

In my high school years, so long ago, many of my classes were activity-based. Mrs. Brennan, in Science, had us working in pairs and in fours throughout the entire year in her lab, conducting experiments and writing them up with careful diagrams and notes—in India ink no less! Mr. Philips, in Physics, used a similar classroom dynamic, with small groups conducting procedures and then sharing results. Mrs. Brooks had us reading plays and poetry aloud in groups, and Mr. Adario used conversational strategies throughout French class. I can't remember anyone having time to be restless and bored, but you might think that involving students in a variety of activities is easier said than done. I agree. But my teachers did it.

E. Building a Literacy Community

18. My mother wants you to phone her.

Connecting the home, the school and the community

The more parents know about the school, and the more teachers know about the home, the greater the chance of developing the child's print power. Michael, Jay's [Grade 4] teacher, came for dinner. (I stopped at nothing to ensure my son's success!) Later over coffee, Jay asked if he could bring down the books he had read to share with Michael. We continued our chat while pile after pile of books from Jay's life covered the rug, and I saw Michael with tears in his eyes. "I never had any books as a child," he whispered. "I was so afraid of them for years and years."

D. B.

Who will our allies be in doing the most for boys with literacy problems? Anyone who can help is the appropriate answer. If there are school staff assigned to these roles, welcome them to your classroom and offer to work with them in designing a richly integrated program that works for both of you and the children. Wherever possible, include them in planning sessions within your classroom community. If students are withdrawn from the class, reorganize the schedule so that the youngsters are gaining, not missing, other meaningful learning experiences. Enlist the librarian's help in supplying suitable books. Work with colleagues to ensure a continuous program of instruction for these children who will need support throughout their school years, developing clear school-wide goals. Share ideas with other teachers, and follow the children's progress from year to year. Make it a school policy to provide guidance for each child for the whole of the child's school life.

Volunteers can read aloud to individuals or groups, listen to children read aloud stories they have written, give book talks, and publish children's writing. You can determine and establish the framework, and volunteers can support its implementation.

Teachers need to develop realistic collaborative goals for working alongside parents. By listening to parents, we can discover a great deal about the family literacy in their homes and incorporate that knowledge into the programs we develop for their children. We can communicate during interviews, by phone calls, or by a classroom newsletter to make them aware of how our programs function and how they can give appropriate support. We can discuss how to assist a troubled reader, why a child needs to read a book silently before sharing it aloud, how to chat with their child about their own reading and writing, how to find a quiet time for reading, how to extend the range of literacy events in the family setting with TV guides or by writing weekly menus, how to use the classroom and public libraries to locate books to read aloud (perhaps by a babysitter or older sibling).

We need to involve parents wherever possible, without adding guilt or stress to their lives, in all aspects of their children's literacy progress. However, we must remember that most are not trained teachers and that the reading and writing experiences at home should be natural and positive. Homework is often a troubling time for boys struggling with literacy. We need to be aware of the demands we place on these children, and offer parents specific and clear suggestions towards understanding what must be achieved each night and how those tasks will support growth in reading and writing. We need to value parents as partners in the education of their children.

As a staff, you could develop a "homework curriculum," a carefully constructed rationale outlining the why's and how's of after-school assignments. It is useful to have students help in the writing of this document. Consider the following questions.

- How will each assignment prepare the student for the next class?
- How will it strengthen the skills that have been demonstrated in class?
- How will it help the child to solve problems or make a creative attempt at a problem only touched upon in class?
- How can the assignment make use of the resources of the home or neighborhood?
- How will the homework help the student to engage in a reading or writing task that is clear and achievable?
- In what ways are we helping students to organize their time and prioritize their activities? (Could an unsupervised boy complete his work at his buddy's home?)
- How much is homework overload? How can we monitor the amount of work each teacher demands?
- Is the homework made use of the next day, or is it just "checked off," giving a sense of unimportance to the activity?
- Is the assignment too difficult without support? Have the assignments accrued to where the child gives up in frustration? How can we get the student back on track?

PARENTING SONS

Neil Postman's *The Disappearance of Children*, first published in 1982, still has relevance for every parent. Postman offers insightful comments on the history of the family, on fathers, changed social values, television, literacy, the loss of confidence in parenting and the loss of intimacy, dependence and loyalty in the parent-child relationship. He says that only two social institutions might resist the decline of childhood: the school and the family.

Especially if you are male or the father of a son, you have an essential role to play in strengthening boys' literacy. Find the books that could matter to boys. Place them beside the popular cultural icons they already treasure. Resist mocking what you may have enjoyed yourself all those years ago. Connect and interconnect all these texts to their own lives and where possible to the bigger world. Let them see the bridges to other lives they have not even imagined. Work

The Men They Will Become, *by Eli Newberger, is a useful resource for examining how we can nurture boys into developing character, so they become responsible and positive young men. Of course, parents will want to read these thoughts, but teachers, as well, need to re-examine their own knowledge of child development and their role in the lives of other people's children. I was particularly struck by Newberger's comments on tenacity: his belief that we must continually engage with boys and never give up on any of them. "This may be the greatest child-raising virtue of all" (p. 19).*

After dinner, Jay had asked me to read *Michael Jackson's autobiography,* Moon Walk, *but I was too tired. Later, I managed to finish the* Carp in the Bathtub, *and that seemed to suffice.*

D. B.

against stereotype and move towards archetype. Value and accept boys' responses, and find ways and means to stretch and deepen them. Help them to find their own emotional selves inside the texts we share, in safe ways, together. Stand for all of the literacies in all the forms and shapes they take, mindful of print's own and particular value. Model what you want them to become—print-strong men who believe in equity. Question and wonder about all the texts you meet, and include boys in the tentative process of meaning making. Let them know that there are different types of literate men and that we value all of them.

"Checklist for Parents," on pages 102–103, will provide you with questions and ideas for assessing your role and influence on the boys in your life.

From **The Boy Who Fell into a Book**
by Alyn Ayckbourn

Dad: (off, calling) *Kevin!*
Kevin: (calling) *Dad!*
Dad: Is your light still on?
Kevin: (switching his bedside light off immediately) *No, Dad.*
Dad: It had better not be. It's half past ten, son. Now, go to sleep. I've told you before, if you want to read, read in the daytime.
Kevin: Yes, Dad.
Dad: Goodnight then, son.
Kevin: Goodnight, Dad. (He waits a few seconds, listening. When he thinks the coast is clear, he reaches out and switches on the light again.)
Dad: (immediately) *Kevin!*
   Kevin switches off the light swiftly.
I won't tell you again!
Kevin: I was just—looking for the light switch, Dad.
Dad: Go to sleep.

Pause. Kevin puts the book away on his bedside shelf alongside five others.
Kevin: How can I go to sleep in the middle of a story? I can't go to sleep till I know what happens to Rockfist. He could be dying. He's trapped in an oven. There mightn't be enough air in there. He could suffocate. Or maybe they'll light the oven. Then he'd be roasted to death. (He ponders.) *or they could flood it with water, or gas or . . . anything . . . the trouble is . . . with a book, it's not like a film . . . with a book . . . a good book . . . it's up here, inside your head . . . and you're like . . . inside the book . . . it becomes part of you . . . real . . . really real . . . really . . . really . . . really . . . real . . .*

Checklist for Parents

☐ Does your son see you as a reader?

☐ Do you occasionally refer to the books on your night table so that your son recognizes you as a reader?

☐ Are there reading materials lying around the house where a boy might notice and peruse them?

☐ Do you bring work literacies home, allowing your son to see you reading and writing for a purpose?

☐ Are you careful never to grill or tease your son about his reading selections?

☐ Can you read the newspaper with your son, so that you can both move into shared reading and discussion about articles?

☐ Do you clip articles of interest and pin them on the fridge door?

☐ Are there other men in your son's life that can offer mentoring as readers, perhaps a grandfather, uncle, coach, or neighbor?

☐ Can you think of a way to let your son know that there are "proud masculine readers" in your social network?

☐ Do you give books, book vouchers or magazine subscriptions as gifts and encourage others in your son's life to do the same?

☐ Do you support your son's library or bookstore choices, even though you might think the titles are too simple, too difficult, or not what you'd expect?

☐ Do you build on your son's interest in a topic through "book sets"? For example, if he is reading a book about a sports figure, you could augment that with information books, books full of records and statistics, and columns from the newspaper.

☐ Do you read aloud interesting tidbits at the dinner table, or share background in the newspaper for a TV show you are going to watch?

☐ When your son is buying gifts for others, do you suggest that he include a book? For example, a book on soccer with a soccer ball.

❑ Do you and your son play board games that require and celebrate word play—Scrabble, Pictionary, and Balderdash. The conversation around the game will be as important as the game itself.

❑ Do you encourage correspondence by post card, letter, and e-mail? Boys need to behave like writers in their everyday lives.

❑ Do you realize that reading aloud can be a dangerous activity for many boys? If you're tempted to pounce on errors, move to silent reading, followed by gentle discussion.

❑ Do you seek out stories and books that your son might not choose himself, but that will enrich his experiences?

❑ Do you set aside 15 minutes at least once a week so that you and your son can enjoy a bit of shared text?

❑ Is there a time in your home when reading is valued over other media, when the whole house shuts down for half an hour?

❑ Does your family see car trips as an opportunity for read-alouds or taped books?

❑ Have you taken time to notice your son's computer efforts? Printing out the screen can let both of you see what has or hasn't been accomplished. How can you help him make his work stronger?

❑ Do you play computer games with your son? Play-based literacies promote other types of reading and writing and allow for the development of social skills within joy-filled activities.

In Jim Giles' primary classroom, a home-school program, called Book and Backpack, was implemented to address a concern by some parents about appropriate homework procedures. Giles was concerned about the idea of having children become actively engaged in the reading process with family members and decided to include a writing component to the homework in a backpack strategy. He purchased three durable backpacks which were filled with paper, pencils, markers, and crayons. The class was organized into nine groups with three children in each group. Everyone was assigned to a specific backpack which was rotated through the group members.

The expectation for B & B was for each child to share a book or magazine that was chosen from the classroom library with a family member. The children were invited to respond to the book in some way, through talk, writing, drawing or creating. Some children wrote letters to their classmates about the story, some wrote stories patterned on the book they read, and some created tape recordings of book talks they had with mothers, fathers or older siblings. Each child who had the duty of taking the backpack home was required to share something with their classmates the next morning.

Larry Swartz

I had to examine my own perceptions when I volunteered at a downtown literacy centre.

I was apprehensive about meeting my student, Darcy. He, however, was the one about to bare his soul. Over the next few months, I came to understand how profoundly illiteracy had affected his life. Darcy was doubly burdened because he concealed his inability to read and write. He lived in constant fear of his children uncovering his secret. He memorized lists and made crude illustrations so he could buy groceries and run errands. He counted subway stops and relied on visual cues when driving. He complained of a sore hand so that the bank teller would fill out his deposit slip. He invented excuses to avoid helping his children with their homework. I could not fathom his exhaustion, his desperation, his shame.*

Darcy's private anguish sharply contrasted the more observable aspects of his life. He had been employed at the Oakville Ford plant for the past eight years. He was a homeowner. He was a caring father to his nine-year-old daughter and seven-year-old son. He had just celebrated his twelfth wedding anniversary. He had a supportive wife who helped him cope with what Darcy called, "the monkey on [his] back." He was only thirty years old, but seemed to have lived a lifetime.

Darcy could not read an issue of Popular Mechanics, *but he could certainly "read" an automobile. He was fascinated by vintage cars. Darcy rescued their carcasses from scrap yards and restored them to their former glory. It was like a spiritual resurrection each time. He showed me albums full of photographs documenting every step* of the restoration process. I was bewildered by most of his explanations and awestruck by his expertise. I could not distinguish a spark plug from a radiator cap. Darcy could build a car from scratch.*

When we abandon narrow interpretations of literacy, we can perceive it in a more accessible and inclusive way. Darcy was literate in auto mechanics and many other texts long before he read a newspaper or wrote a cheque. Like most people who had difficulty with print literacy, he was capable of learning to read and write. Unlike most, he sought help despite feelings of inadequacy and embarrassment. Darcy shattered my preconceptions. His honesty and courage led me to redefine my concept of literacy.

Literacy volunteer

I found myself having a cup of coffee with both Jeremy's parents in the house they rented. Jeremy's father looked rather rough, with a Harley-Davidson shirt and a plethora of tattoos on his arms. The reality was that they were both very friendly. They were uncomfortable with reading to and with Jeremy, but said they would make an effort to encourage and listen to Jeremy as best they could . . .

Jeremy is now in the middle of reading Phantom of the Opera *and is genuinely excited about his future. Jeremy, his parents and I watched the movie version of* The Secret Garden *and Jeremy gave a simple critique: "The book was better."*

Student teacher

19. I don't like any of these books.

Building literacy and literature resources for boys

Jay spent two hours following directions to create a hopping frog, bravely interrupting my own work to confer on a difficult set of directions. I was of no help, and even less support, and yet he figured it out and his frog indeed hopped. (As did the following ten he secretly set in motion in my doorway.)

How do they do it? How do children come to make sense of instructions so unclear and so complex? I will keep the first frog. On my desk, for strength when the task seems too difficult. To nudge me when I can't find time to explain, clarify, restate unclear directions to a child. Folded frogs from fabulous fingers asking eyes to follow the print tracks on the white page. Why does expository print take such a back seat in reading teaching, relegated to writing a description on how to fix a flat bicycle tire or tie a shoe?

D. B.

The issue of what boys read needs to be considered carefully, always bearing in mind that there is no one category of boys or of what they read. However, we can use research—surveys and questionnaires, interviews and observations, and sales figures and library statistics—to help us paint a general picture of what many, if not most, boys read or would read if they could.

So many factors help determine what materials boys read. We know that boys' reading interests are affected by their age, gender, culture, reading ability, background, parents, peers, availability of materials, and, of course, by the media.

Voluntary reading, or "life reading," is usually done outside school, feeding boys' developing interests. Much of this reading remains outside adult control and selection, but when it is looked at more closely, we find out that boys are reading so much more than many adults realize—comic books, novels in adventure and horror series, jokes and riddles, instructions for toys and games, the fact-filled cards they collect and, of course, the computer screen.

How should we accommodate "life reading" resources in school, or should "school reading" remain disconnected? Some educators are very concerned about this separation. They fear that boys will devalue books as adults because of this divide. Certainly our interviews established that many men choose not to read books. They stated that for them, school reading consisted of enforced reading of long, difficult books with extended passages of text that held little interest, never mind textbooks written with an absence of story or emotion, or often, style.

We know that classroom activities and instructional methods and materials have to be considered if we want to help boys see reading as an authentic and useful life process.

- Can we choose materials that boys as well as girls will consider relevant to their needs and interests? Results from one study indicate that boys are less satisfied than girls with the books offered to them in the primary classroom; girls' choices of books tended to coincide with those of their teachers. What resources have we put in place for boys who are reluctant readers (sometimes the same students labeled as "gifted")?

- Research has shown that the motivation for reading and literature can be increased if it is incorporated into other curriculum areas, such as drama, science, and social studies. As students explore topics of interest to them, they are required to read for informational purposes. Similarly, classroom events that support the sharing of books and reading experiences with others can promote reading and literature. There, boys "talk their way" into becoming aware of other literacy materials through peer group interactions and meet new books chosen around their interests and abilities in book talks given by teachers, librarians and other students.

REMEMBERING TO READ ALOUD

Picture books and anthologies are often forgotten as read-aloud resources for children in older grades. They shouldn't be. See "Read-aloud resources" and "Picture books" under Recommended Books for Boys for some powerful examples.

In *Boys' Own*, Tim Wynne-Jones provides young readers with 20 short stories by contemporary Canadian writers. He says that although the book is called *Boys' Own*, he didn't select these stories with a fixed idea of what would work with boys—he chose stories he liked. The stories explore the themes of wilderness survival, sports, and outdoors. They run from being hilarious to dark in mood, for example, Brian Doyle's outstanding contribution "Pincher." And there is a companion book called *Girls' Own*. (It would be interesting to reverse the readership and compare the responses with a class of both boys and girls.) These sophisticated stories zero in on the problems that boys face in their lives at school and at home.

Note how there has been a resurgence of myths, as video games, TV shows and CD-ROMs incorporate their elements into contemporary settings. Could that phenomenon spark more interest in reading the stories? Consider, too, folk tales, or "the stories of the tribe." The context of "long ago" enables the child to explore universal problems and concerns that have troubled humanity forever, but in a safe, non-threatening framework. The deeds of heroes, the schemes of tricksters, and the lore of nations past can all serve as settings for the child's own development through family situations, societal difficulties, supernatural beliefs, and natural phenomena.

ENTICING BOYS TO READ

> ***From* The Adventures of Captain Underpants**
> *by Dav Pilkey*
>
> *"Mommy," said a little boy sitting on a bench, "I just saw two robots driving a van with a guy in his underwear hanging off the back by a red cape, pulling two boys on skateboards behind him with his feet."*
> *"How do you expect me to believe such a ridiculous story?" asked his mother.*

Hasn't Dav Pilkey invented the perfect character to capture the attention of young readers who are drawn to off-the-wall adventure? Who would turn down the chance to read about a character named

The Amazing Captain Underpants? The rollicking sense of humor, the comic book format, the visual jokes in Pilkey's drawings, and the subversive undertone of the Captain Underpants series are sure-fire winners for Grades 3 and 4 boys who are reluctant to read. The titles alone lure young readers to grab these hilarious books. The characters, George and Harold, are fourth graders with an uncontrollable silly streak that prompts assorted pranks and mayhem. They spend each afternoon creating comic books featuring Captain Underpants and sell the comics at school for 50 cents apiece.

With the wealth of children's books today, no boy need begin reading with limited, meaningless, vocabulary-controlled readers. Depending on the experiences of the child, books for the beginning reader can explore and depict all aspects of life and language. The more difficult words, such as "stegosaurus" and "dinosaur," are easily understood when the story gives the child the necessary context for understanding the print.

Beginning books for young readers cover a wide range: concept books with labels and lists; short sentences that explain or illuminate the picture; easy-read books, written by fine authors but with simple vocabulary; and picture books with a minimal number of lines and words. The Frog and Toad books by Arnold Lobel will always be my favorite books to introduce to reluctant boy readers. Popular easy-read series are identified under Recommended Books for Boys.

Ready-to-read books give young readers an opportunity to sustain their reading over a longer period of time. Whether the book is a series of short stories about the same characters, or a series of sequential chapters that create a complete story, it will give children a chance to anticipate and predict: the major thinking operations in reading. As the incidents and images grow one upon the other, children build a larger framework for understanding and may come to realize the pleasure and satisfaction that comes from "a longer read."

The operative word for success is humor. The popular books are funny, often silly, with illogical events piling up, upside-down humans alongside weird creatures, lots of wordplay—puns and riddles—and a calculated sense of the taboo topics, like the infamous underwear.

MOVING INTO NOVELS

Jane O'Connor, of Penguin Putnam's Mass Merchandise Group, said her son once told her he would read any book that had "weird" or "chocolate" in the title. "Boys need books that match their level of sophistication as far as humor and what they're into and still are relatively easy to read. That's why we've kept on doing The Zack Files. *The boys in the books are fifth-graders, but the books are written at a high second-grade level."*

From Tut Tut
by Jon Scieszka

Now before things get out of hand (and you know they will as soon as we land), I'd like to take a minute to explain a few things.

First of all—I had no idea what I was getting into when my Uncle Joe gave me The Book for my birthday. It turns out that this is no ordinary book. This thing is a time machine. Every time we open it, it takes us to a

> *different time. Which sounds like great fun. But there is one little prob-*
> *lem. The only way to get back to our time is to find The Book in the other*
> *time. And whenever we time travel, The Book has a nasty habit of disap-*
> *pearing.*
>
> *We've gotten in trouble for looking for The Book in King Arthur's*
> *court, on Blackbeard's pirate ship, in a stone-age cave, and in places*
> *you don't even want to know about.*
>
> *So you think by now we would have figured out how to use The Book*
> *without losing it. Well . . . we haven't. And if you've got any bright ideas*
> *of what we should do—keep them to yourself.*

The Time Warp Trio series appeals especially to boys who want to read fiction, but haven't found many books they like. The stories are fast-paced reads, blending adventure, humor, magic and slapstick. The mindset of typical young boys is captured in the dialogue and interactions of the three main characters: level-headed Joe, brainy Sam, and goofy Fred. Each book takes the students to another time and place (e.g., Greece (*It's All Greek to Me*), Egypt (*Tut Tut*), medieval times (*Knights of the Kitchen Table*) so that the readers learn facts about living outside the contemporary world. The research should to be taken with grain of salt, though, since the main purpose of these books is to entertain.

First novels mark a reading plateau for young independent readers, now able to sustain their interest over several chapters, make sense of plot and characters, and find aesthetic pleasure in the wholeness of the longer story. Boys may enjoy reading a series of novels by one author, discovering more about familiar characters. Or, they may read several novels on a theme, such as mystery or humor. It is important that they not be pushed into reading novels that don't interest them or that they find too difficult, for success in this phase in their reading growth may determine their futures as readers. I am nervous about the growing trend to having the whole class reading copies of a single novel. Have we provided support for those children having difficulties? Have we chosen the book for a specific purpose?

The personal and private reading of a novel gives a boy the security to delve into situations that may touch his life, permitting him to identify and reflect on his development, his concern about his place in the adult world, ecology, peace, the future, or the past. We must appreciate the need that these young readers have for understanding life's problems and accept that the portrayal and examination of these issues, carefully and artfully developed in the novel form, will strengthen their understanding and beliefs.

Because of their well-developed reading abilities and mature interests, some boys may want to move into adult novels early. However, there are books written especially for mature, young readers; these sophisticated, sensitive works of art deserve a place in boys' lives. Such books allow boys to focus on issues that affect them at their own emotional level, but also stretch their minds and imaginations and present them with complicated and interlocking structures for deep learning, as well.

Recommended Books for Boys notes appealing series for young and older boys, as well as engaging novels for both groups.

PLAYING WITH WORDS

Teachers can use young children's inherent love of the sounds of language to create a climate in which children enjoy and find satisfaction in acquiring word power. As well, playful and adventurous experiences with words can contribute to a better understanding of the technical aspects of the complexities of language—the spellings, sounds, rhythms, and incongruities of this complex and vital communication system. In *Babushka's Mother Goose*, for example, Patricia Polacco presents rhymes and stories as told by her Russian grandmother. Words like Natasha, Ivana, Katushka, and Babushka delight the listening children, who are involved in the sounds of language from the very first page.

See "Word play books" under Recommended Books for Boys for some strong examples.

RETHINKING WHAT POETRY IS

Reading the poems of young Mattie Stepanek, whose two anthologies have made best-seller lists, you cannot help but rejoice at the power of poetic language to harness and give shape to our deepest emotions and thoughts.

We may need to rethink the definition of poetry. When we follow tight rules about form and content, we lose the very boys we may be trying to reach. One high school student told me not long ago that he once thought all poems had to rhyme. James Britton popularized the term *poetic writing*, and freed us from "worse verse"—the writings of children struggling to follow a shape that neither suited their content nor revealed any developing skills. Michael Rosen and others changed our perceptions further. They wrote wonderful monologues and dialogues, labeled them poetry, and opened the eyes of many adults and children to writing from feeling. (Find Rosen's anthologies and you will have dozens of literacy experiences to share with boys.)

Today, when poetry anthologies and songbooks abound, boys can choose from all types to fill their particular interests. Some of the books are beautifully illustrated, while others depend on the strength of the imagination. Authors select past favorites, often adapting or rewriting them, and use well-known patterns on which to build new ideas and create wonderful new sounds and images to delight children through the ear. The language structure and vocabulary that are embedded in poems and songs give power for future meaning making with print.

Check out "Easy-read poetry," "Poetry for young boys" and "Poetry for older boys" under Recommended Books for Boys. You will find many excellent resources.

Boys love the ghoulish, the gross and the disgusting. Yet how often is this allowed to appear in children's books? When it does, it is carefully sanitised so as not to offend adult sensibilities. Almost every title that has ever attempted to make story out of the messy, the uncouth and the horrible that so fascinates boys has attracted criticism or outright bans.

Should we fret about this? No. Here is an even greater heresy. A story is words on a page. Reading it involves decoding those words to make meaning. Perceptions of quality are judgements applied arbitrarily on top of this. What adults value in a book is not necessarily what boys value in a book. It does not have to be the same, either, except in one vital aspect. If we are to address reluctance to read, both adults and boys must value material that boys do want to read. Adults must be prepared to let boys walk amongst familiar territory before they are asked to run amid the richness that the wider adult world offers. There is plenty of scope for that amongst the books read TO boys.

This is how we build a culture of books and reading amongst our boys. As they mature towards manhood, their fascination for the ghoulish and disgusting will wane but what will proceed into manhood with the boys is a culture of reading established and nourished through the years of boyhood.

James Moloney

He [Stanley] recited the alphabet for Zero, then Zero repeated it without a single mistake.

Not bad for a kid who had never seen Sesame Street.

"Well, I've heard it before, somewhere," Zero said, trying to act like it was nothing, but his big smile gave him away.

The next step was harder. Stanley had to figure out how to teach him to recognize each letter. He gave Zero a piece of paper, and took a piece for himself. "I guess we'll start with A."

From Holes,
by Louis Sachar

Sometimes I feel like I have walked into the middle of a movie. It is a strange movie with no plot and no beginning. The movie is in black and white, and grainy. Sometimes the camera moves in so close that you can't tell what is going on and you just listen to the sounds and guess. I have seen movies of prisons but never one like this. This is not a movie about bars and locked doors. It is about being alone when you are not really alone and about being scared all the time.

I think to get used to this I will have to give up what I think is real and take up something else. I wish I could make sense of it.

Maybe I could make my own movie. I could write it out and play it in my head. I could block out the scenes like we did in school. The film will be the story of my life. No, not my life, but of this experience. I'll write it down in the notebook they let me keep. I'll call it what the lady who is the prosecutor called me. M O N S T E R.

From Monster,
by Walter Dean Myers

Bringing Boys into Literacy

Do schools (and parents) unconsciously discriminate against many boys in their attempts at becoming literate?

What resources do we select for boys and girls to read?

What responses do we value most from children who are discussing their stories with us?

How do we ourselves react to boys' and girls' literacy behaviors?

Do we reinforce socially constructed frames of being a boy or a girl, or do we help youngsters to expand on or to redefine them?

How do we handle male peer groups who pressure others in the class to respond in "stereotypical male" fashion to ideas that are shared?

Do we encourage different ways of participating in print-focused contexts, modeling and demonstrating alternative possibilities for literacy behaviors?

Do we make explicit the stereotypes that the media (and society) throw up about what men and women are expected to read?

Do we open up response discussions so that boys and girls can note the different ways of becoming a reader and a writer?

Can we help boys extend who they are, and alter their life's directions through their reading of others' lives, accepting the challenges that books offer to their own becomings?

Why do so many boys and girls construct their images of being a reader and a writer in very different ways?

What role does gender play in this definition of a literacy self? Are girls, too, confirming their gender identities by conforming to the norms of their peer groups in choosing to read certain books and to write about particular issues? From the observations and research of several teachers, parents, and researchers, reading (and to a degree, writing) appears to reflect and affirm gender identity.

If reading "reflects and confirms" gender, can we use that influence on behaviors in boys and girls to see gender issues through a critical lens?

Are we as teachers and parents powerless over peer group pressures? Why is it that some classrooms are able to extend the literacy behaviors and constructs of so many boys and girls? Why are these effective changes happening in some schools, regardless of their socio-economic contexts?

Boys and Books: No Leftovers

In his compelling novel *Loser*, Jerry Spinelli builds a picture of one boy over six years at school. This boy's life is riddled with bad luck and misfortune. I still ache when I remember the story, and any of us who have taught or been labeled "loser" know this boy from the inside out.

That we who live alongside boys forget or aren't able to bring them to powerful books fills me with sadness. Although the media put so much emphasis on monitoring films, videos, CDs and computers, I hear little about selecting books written for boys who are at particular ages and stages in their lives.

If we want literate young men who think critically and deeply about all the texts they will experience, we need to provide them with events worthy of being included in their education at home and at school. That a boy never meets a book that pulls him inside until he can barely breathe should not happen in our print-rich society. We have so many gifted writers helping us to raise our boys alongside our girls as thoughtful, aware, articulate and compassionate citizens.

Read this excerpt from *Loser* and remember this boy's strength forever. He knew he was as worthy as any of his teammates, and he stood his ground until they knew it too. Just as Jay did. A hockey player through and through.

And, of course, we all know that even hockey players read.

From Loser
by Jerry Spinelli

They go choosing sides—Tuttles here, Bonces here—until the only one left is Zinkoff in the yellow hat. But the sides are even. Tuttle and Bonce have each chosen seven kids. Yellow hat is a leftover.

But this kid's not acting like a leftover. A normal leftover would see that he's one too many, that everybody but him has been picked and that therefore he must be pretty hopeless and therefore he better just get on out of there and go play something he's good at like Monopoly.

But this kid just stands there. He shows no sign of turning and vanishing. And he's not just standing there, he's staring at Tuttle and Bonce.

Tuttle says, "We got enough."

So now the kid is just staring at Bonce. And Bonce wants to say "We got enough," but he can't seem to say it. He wishes the kid would just turn and go away. Doesn't he know he's a leftover?

Hobin's voice rings out from the other side: "Tackle!"

They usually play two-hand tag. There are no pads, no helmets. And half the field is muddy from the melted snow. But no one objects. No one wants to appear to be afraid to tackle.

Janski speaks: "The sides are even up. We don't need nobody else."

The kid does not take the hint.

This is uncharted territory: a leftover who won't go away. Still, Bonce holds the power. All he has to do is open his mouth. Please, go, *he thinks. The kid is still staring at Bonce. The kid really is stupid. The kid doesn't know that even if he's allowed in he's only going to be ignored. Or embarrassed. Or hurt. He doesn't know that he's a klutz. Doesn't know he's out of his league.*

Doesn't know a leftover doesn't stare down a chooser. Doesn't know he's supposed to look down at his shoes or up at the sky and wish he could disappear, because that's what he is, a leftover, the last kid left.

But this kid won't back off, and his stare is hitting Bonce like a football in the forehead. In those eyes Bonce sees something he doesn't understand, and something else he dimly remembers. . . .

This is goofy, *he thinks,* He thinks of a thousand things to say, a thousand other ways this could go, but in the end there's really only one word, he knows that, one word from him and who knows where we go from there?

He points, he says it: "Zinkoff."

And the game begins.

Interview Questions

- Do you visit the school library? When?

- How often do you go to the library?

- What do you prefer to read? Fiction? Non-fiction?

- Do you read for homework every night?

- Do people buy you books? Do you like people buying you books for birthdays and holidays?

- Does anyone read to you at home?
  Mom   Dad   Grandma   Grandpa   Brother   Sister   Someone else

- Do they read to you in English or another language?

- Do the men in your house read? What do they read?
  Newspapers   Fiction   Magazines   Non-fiction   Religious books

- Do you like reading?

- How important is reading to you?

- Who reads more? Boys? Girls? Both the same?

- Do you know what kinds of books your friends like?

- Do you know someone in your class who is a really good reader?

- Do you discuss books with the other kids?

- How did you learn to read?

- How would you describe yourself as a reader?

- Do you write letters to other people?

- Do you play games on the computer?

- Do you use a computer when you write?

- Do you prefer to use a pen or pencil?

- Do you print or do cursive writing?

- Do you like to read some stories more than once?

- Do you think textbooks are hard to read?

- Do you have a book collection at home? Do you borrow or trade books with your friends?

- How much television do you watch a day? With whom do you watch television?

- What do you like to do in your spare time?

- Do you have any brothers or sisters?

- If you had children, what would you want them to read?

- What kinds of words do you find difficult to read?

- What do you do when you can't read a word?

- Do you look at the pictures in books while you're reading?

- What do you want to be when you grow up? What will you need to read to do that job?

- What kinds of stories bother you the most?

- Do you enjoy listening to your teacher read aloud?

- Do you play games where you have to read, like Monopoly?

- Do you have a favorite book? Do you have a favorite author?

- Are reading assignments in school worthwhile?

- Are reading tests fair?

- What advice do you have for Language Arts teachers today?

- What could your teacher do to make reading more enjoyable for you?

- What do you remember about the experience of learning to read?

- What do you read on a regular basis?

- Have you ever recommended a book to someone else to read?

- Do you ever re-read a favorite book or article?

- What section of a bookstore do you go to first?

- What do you choose to read at home?

- What do you choose to read at school?

- What do you like to read about?

- What kinds of activities do you like to do in school?

Recommended Books for Boys

READ-ALOUD RESOURCES

Aesop's Fables, by Jerry Pinkney

The Arabian Nights, by Brian Alderson

A Barrel of Laughs, A Vale of Tears, by Jules Feiffer

Beware! R. L Stine Picks His Favorite Scary Stories, by R. L. Stine

Boys' Own, edited by Tim Wynne-Jones

Caribou Song, by Tomson Highway

Casey at the Bat, by Ernest Lawrence Thayer and Christopher Bing

The Cat and the Wizard, by Dennis Lee

Charlotte's Web, by E. B. White (Also: *Stuart Little*, *The Trumpet of the Swan*)

The Crane Wife, by Odds Bodkin

Crow and Weasel, by Tom Pohrt

The Dark Thirty: Southern Tales of the Supernatural, by Patricia McKissack

The Day of Ahmed's Secret, by Florence Parry Heide and Judith Heide Gilliland

Dead Man's Gold: And Other Stories, by Paul Yee

The Dumb Bunnies, by Dav Pilkey (Also: *The Dumb Bunnies' Easter*, *The Dumb Bunnies Go to the Zoo*, *Make Way for the Dumb Bunnies*)

The Dust Bowl, by David Booth

The Elders Are Watching, by David Bouchard (Also: *Buddha in the Garden*, *The Great Race*, *If You're Not from the Prairie*)

Enchantment: Fairy Tales, Ghost Stories and Tales of Wonder, by Kevin Crossley-Holland

Encounter, by Jane Yolen

Eric Carle's Treasury of Classic Stories for Children, by Eric Carle

Fables, by Arnold Lobel

Fox, by Margaret Wild

Frederick's Fables, by Leo Lionni

From Sea to Shining Sea: A Treasury of American Folklore and Folksongs, edited by Amy Cohn

The Ghost-Eye Tree, by Bill Martin Jr. and John Archambault

The Ghost Horse of the Mounties, by Sean O'Huigin

Ghost Train, by Paul Yee

The Girl Who Loved the Wind, by Jane Yolen

The Half-a-Moon Inn, by Paul Fleischman

Her Stories: African American Folktales, Fairy Tales and True Tales, by Virginia Hamilton

I Am Arachne: Fifteen Greek and Roman Myths, by Elizabeth Spires

I Am the Dog / I Am the Cat, by Donald Hall

The Iron Man, by Ted Hughes (Sequel: *The Iron Woman*)

Joseph Had a Little Overcoat, by Simms Taback

Just So Stories, by Rudyard Kipling

King Kong, by Anthony Browne

Life Doesn't Frighten Me at All, by Maya Angelou

The Little Old Lady Who Was Not Afraid of Anything, by Linda Williams

Lon Po Po: A Red Riding Hood Story from China, by Ed Young (Also: *Cat and Rat: The Legend of the Chinese Zodiac*)

The Lost Children, by Paul Goble (Also: *Crow Chief*, *Death of the Iron Horse*, *Dream Wolf*, *The Girl Who Loved Wild Horses*, Iktomi (Series), *Love Flute*, *Star Boy*)

Mr. Lincoln's Way, by Patricia Polacco (Also: *Chicken Sunday*, *The Keeping Quilt*, *Pink and Say*, *Rachenka's Eggs*, *Thank You Mr. Falker*)

The Orphan Boy, by Tololwa Mollel

Owl Moon, by Jane Yolen

Pecos Bill, by Steven Kellogg (Also: *The Day Jimmy's Boa Ate the Wash*, *The Island of the Skogg*, *Mysterious Tadpole*, *Paul Bunyan*, *Pinkerton*)

The People Could Fly: American Black Folktales, by Virgina Hamilton

The Polar Express, by Chris Van Allsburg

Riding the Tiger, by Eve Bunting (Also: *Fly Away Home*, *Gleam and Glow*, *Train to Somewhere*, *The Wall*, *Your Move*)

Round Trip, by Ann Jonas

Scary Stories to Tell in the Dark (Series), by Alvin Schwartz

The Seals on the Bus, by Lenny Hort

Smoky Night, by Eve Bunting

Snow White in New York, by Fiona French

Squids Will Be Squids, by Jon Scieszka (Also: *The Frog Prince Continued*, *The Stinky Cheese Man and Other Fairly Stupid Tales*, *The True Story of the Three Little Pigs*)

Tales from Gold Mountain, by Paul Yee

The Three Questions, by Jon Muth

Tiger, by Judy Allen (Also: *Elephant, Panda, Seal, Whale*)

The True Story of Trapper Jack's Big Toe, by Ian Wallace (Also: *Boy of the Deeps, Duncan's Way, The Name of the Tree, The Very Last First Time*)

Twelve Shots: Outstanding Short Stories about Guns, by Harry Mazer

The Very Kind Rich Lady and Her One Hundred Dogs, by Chinlun Lee

The Very Persistent Gappers of Fripp, by George Saunders

Weasel, by Cynthia De Felice

Wingwalker, by Rosemary Wells

The Wolf at the Door and Other Retold Fairy Tales, edited by Ellen Datlow and Terri Windling

Yeh Shen: A Cinderella Story from China, by Louie Ai-Ling

You Read to Me, I'll Read to You: Very Short Stories to Read Together, by Mary Ann Hoberman

PICTURE BOOKS

Alexander and the Terrible, Horrible, No Good Very Bad Day, by Judith Viorst

Bark, George!, by Jules Feiffer (Also: *By the Side of the Road*)

The Big Sneeze, by Ruth Brown (Also: *A Dark Dark Tale*)

The Boy of a Thousand Faces, by Brian Selznick

Chicka Chicka Boom Boom, by Bill Martin Jr. and John Archambault

Click, Clack, Moo: Cows That Type, by Doreen Cronin (Also: *Giggle, Giggle, Quack*)

Dinosaur Cousins, by Bernard Most (Also: *Whatever Happened to the Dinosaurs?, If the Dinosaurs Came Back*)

Doctor De Soto, by William Steig

Doctor Dog, by Babette Cole

Edward and the Pirates, by David McPhail

The Everything Book, by Denise Fleming (Also: *Barnyard Banter, In the Small Small Pond, Lunch*)

The First Dog, by Jan Brett

Frederick, by Leo Lionni (Also: *Alexander and the Wind-up Mouse, The Biggest House in the World, Fish Is Fish, Little Blue and Little Yellow, Swimmy, Tillie and the Wall*)

The Gingerbread Boy, by Paul Galdone

Good News! Bad News!, by Colin McNaughton

The Hockey Sweater, by Roch Carrier

If You Take a Mouse to School, by Laura Numeroff (Also: *If You Give a Mouse a Cookie, If You Give a Pig a Pancake, If You Take a Mouse to the Movies*)

In My World, by Lois Ehlert (Also: *Fish Eyes, Growing Vegetable Soup, Market Day, Moon Rope, Planting a Rainbow, Snowballs, Waiting for Wings*)

Jumanji, by Chris Van Allsburg (Also: *The Garden of Abdul Gasazi, The Mysteries of Harris Burdick, The Polar Express, The Stranger, Two Bad Ants, The Widow's Broom, The Wretched Stone, The Z Was Zapped*)

McBroom's Wonderful One-Acre Farm, by Sid Fleischman

Miss Nelson Is Missing, by Harry Allard (Also: *Miss Nelson Is Back, Miss Nelson Has a Field Day*)

Miss Bindergarten Gets Ready for Kindergarten, by Joseph Slate (Also: *Miss Bindergarten Celebrates the 100th Day of Kindergarten, Miss Bindergarten Stays Home from Kindergarten*)

Mister Magnolia, by Quentin Blake (Also: *All Join In, Clown, Simpkin, Zagazoo*)

No, David! (Trilogy), by David Shannon (Sequels: *David Gets in Trouble, David Goes to School*)

No Jumping on the Bed, by Todd Arnold (Also: *Parts, More Parts*)

Nonsense! He Yelled, by Roger Eschbacher

Off We Go!, by Jane Yolen

One Fish Two Fish Red Fish Blue Fish, by Dr. Seuss (Also: *The Cat in the Hat, The 500 Hats of Bartholomew Cubbins, Green Eggs and Ham, Horton Hatches the Egg, The Lorax*)

Owen, by Kevin Henkes (Also: *Julius and the Baby of the World, A Weekend with Wendell, Wemberly Worried*)

The Paperbag Princess, by Robert Munsch (Also: *From Far Away, Good Families Don't, Pigs*)

Pete's a Pizza, by William Steig

Pigs Aplenty, Pigs Galore!, by David McPhail (Also: *Pigs Ahoy!, Those Can-Do Pigs*)

Polar Bear, Polar Bear, What Do You Hear?, by Bill Martin Jr. (Also: *Brown Bear, Brown Bear, What Do You See?*)

The Principal's New Clothes, by Stephanie Calmenson

Sam's Pizza!, by David Pelham (Also: *Sam's Sandwich, Say Cheese! The Sensational Samburger*)

Seven Blind Mice, by Ed Young

The Silly Goose, by Dav Pilkey (Also: *Dogzilla, Kat Kong, Dog Breath, Hallo-weiner*)

"Slowly, Slowly, Slowly," said the Sloth, by Eric Carle (Also: *Do You Want to Be My Friend?, From Head to Toe, The Grouchy Ladybug, Hello Red Fox, The Very Quiet Cricket, The Very Hungry Caterpillar*)

The Snowman, by Raymond Briggs (Also: *The Man*)

Starry Messenger, by Peter Sis

Stellaluna, by Janell Cannon (Also: *Crickwing, Trupp, Verdi*)

This Is the House That Jack Built, by Simms Taback (Also: *There Was an Old Lady Who Swallowed a Fly*)

The Three Pigs, by David Wiesner (Also: *Tuesday*)

Tough Boris, by Mem Fox

Voices in the Park, by Anthony Browne (Also: *Changes, Gorilla, My Dad, Piggybook, The Tunnel, Zoo*)

Yo! Yes!, by Chris Raschka (Also: *Ring! Yo?*)

Where the Forest Meets the Sea, by Jeanne Baker (Also: *The Story of Rosy Dock, Window*)

Where the Wild Things Are, by Maurice Sendak (Also: *Chicken Soup with Rice, In the Night Kitchen*)

Wilfrid Gordon McDonald Partridge, by Mem Fox

William's Doll, by Charlotte Zolotow

The Winter Hole, by Graeme Base

Would You Rather . . ., by John Burningham (Also: *Cloudland, Mr. Gumpy's Outing, Mr. Gumpy's Motor Car, Where's Julius?*)

Za-Za's Baby Brother, by Lucy Cousins

EASY-READ SERIES

Amelia Bedelia, by Peggy Parish

Arthur, by Marc Brown

Curious George, by H. A. Rey

The Cut-ups, by James Marshall

Days with Frog and Toad, by Arnold Lobel (Also: *Mouse Soup, Mouse Tales, Owl at Home, Uncle Elephant*)

Franklin, by Paulette Bourgeois

George and Martha: The Complete Stories of Two Best Friends, by James Marshall

Henry and Mudge, by Cynthia Rylant

The Kids of the Polk Street School, by Patricia Reilly Giff

Marvin Redpost, by Louis Sachar

Nate the Great, by Marjorie Weinman Sharman

The Stupids, by Harry Allard

Willy the Champ, by Anthony Browne

SERIES FOR YOUNG BOYS

A to Z Mysteries, by Ron Roy

The Adventures of the Bailey School Kids, by Debbie Dadey and Marcia Thornton Jones

The Adventures of Captain Underpants, by Dav Pilkey

Barkley's School for Dogs, by Marcia Thornton Jones and Debbie Dadey

Bunnicula, by James and Deborah Howe

Cam Jansen, by David A. Adler

The Culpepper Adventures, by Gary Paulsen

Dinotopia, by Peter David

Encyclopedia Brown, by Donald J. Sobol

The Hardy Boys: All New Adventures, by Franklin W. Dixon

The Magic Shop Books, by Bruce Colville

The Magic Tree House, by Mary Pope Osborne

Munschworks: The First Munsch Collection, by Robert Munsch

The Nomes, by Terry Pratchett

Pee Wee Scouts, by Judy Delton

Ricky Ricotta's Mighty Robots, by Dav Pilkey

Sam: Dog Detective, by Mary Labatt

Screech Owls, by Roy MacGregor

A Series of Unfortunate Events, by Lemony Snicket

Sideways Stories from a Wayside School, by Louis Sachar

Soup, by Robert Newton Peck

Star Wars Jedi Apprentice, by Jude Watson (Also: Jedi Quest)

The Time Warp Trio, by Jon Scieszka

The Werewolf Club, by Daniel Pinkwater

SERIES FOR OLDER BOYS

Animorphs, by K. A. Applegate

Choose Your Own Star Wars Adventure, by Christopher Golden

Ever World, by K. A. Applegate

Remnants, by K. A. Applegate

The Book of Three, by Lloyd Alexander

The Chronicles of Narnia, by C. S. Lewis

The Dark Is Rising, by Susan Cooper

Goosebumps, by R. L. Stine
Harry Potter, by J. K. Rowling
I Was a Sixth Grade Werewolf, by Bruce Colville
Tales of Redwall, by Brian Jacques
Swallows and Amazons, by Arthur Ransome
Tom Austen Mysteries, by Eric Wilson
The Wolfbay Wings, by Bruce Brooks

NOVELS FOR YOUNG BOYS

Be a Perfect Person in Just Three Days, by Stephen Manes

The Best Christmas Pageant Ever, by Barbara Robinson (Also: *The Worst Kids in the World*)

Chocolate Fever, by Robert Kimmel Smith (Also: *Jelly Belly, Mostly Michael, The War with Grandpa*)

Coraline, by Neil Gaiman

Dear Mr. Henshaw, by Beverly Cleary (Sequel: *Strider*)

The Field of Dogs, by Katherine Paterson

Fourth Grade Weirdo, by Martha Freeman

From the Mixed-up Files of Mrs. Basil E. Frankweiler, by E. L. Konigsburg

The Giggler Treatment, by Roddy Doyle

The Graduation of Jake Moon, by Barbara Park

The Hoboken Chicken Emergency, by Daniel Manus Pinkwater (Also: *Fat Men from Space, Mush: A Dog from Space*).

Holes, by Louis Sachar

Homer Price, by Robert McCloskey (Also: *Centerburg Tales*)

How to Eat Fried Worms, by Thomas Rockwell

I Was a Rat, by Philip Pullman (Also: *Clockwork, Count Karlstein*)

In the Year of the Boar and Jackie Robinson, by Bette Bao Lord

Island (Trilogy), by Gordon Korman (Also: *Everest*)

Jacob Two-Two Meets the Hooded Fang (Trilogy), by Mordecai Richler

The Jacket, by Andrew Clements (Also: *Frindle, The Landry News, The Janitor's Boy, The School Story*)

James and the Giant Peach, by Roald Dahl (Also: *The BFG, Charlie and the Chocolate Factory, Danny the Champion of the World, George's Marvelous Medicine, Matilda, The Twits, The Witches*)

Joey Pigza Loses Control, by Jack Gantos (Also: *Joey Pigza Swallowed the Key*)

King of Shadows, by Susan Cooper (Also: *The Boggart*)

Loser, by Jerry Spinelli

Love That Dog, by Sharon Creech

Mean Margaret, by Tor Seidler

Mick Harte Was Here, by Barbara Park (Also: *Skinnybones*)

The Mouse and the Motorcycle (Trilogy), by Beverly Cleary (Also: *Ralph S. Mouse, Runaway Ralph*)

Muggie Maggie, by Beverly Cleary

The Nose from Jupiter, by Richard Scrimger (Also: *A Nose for Adventure, Noses are Red*)

Perloo the Bold, by Avi

The Phantom Tollbooth, by Norton Juster

The Pinballs, by Betsy Byars (Also: *Cracker Jackson, The Eighteenth Emergency, The House of Wings, The Midnight Fox, The Summer of the Swans*)

Poppy (Series), by Avi

Rats, by Paul Zindel

Road Trip, by Eric Walters (Also: *Full Court, Hoop Crazy, Long Shot*)

The Sheep Pig (Babe), by Dick King-Smith (Also: *Daggie Dogfoot, The Fox Busters, Harry's Mad, The Mouse Butcher, Pets for Keeps, The Queen's Nose*)

Shiloh (Trilogy), by Phyllis Naylor (Sequels: *Saving Shiloh, Shiloh Season*)

Stone Fox, by John Reynolds Gardiner

The Summer of Riley, by Eve Bunting

Tales of a Fourth Grade Nothing, by Judy Blume (Sequel: *Superfudge*)

A Taste of Blackberries, by Doris B. Smith

This Can't Be Happening at MacDonald Hall, by Gordon Korman (Also: *Beware the Fish, Bruno and Boots, The Chicken Doesn't Skate, Fifth Grade Radio, Our Man Weston, No Coins, Please, Go Jump in the Pool!, Sixth Grade Nickname Game, The War with Mr. Wizzle, The Zucchini Warriors*)

Thank You, Jackie Robinson, by Barbara Cohen

The Tiger Rising, by Kate DiCamillo

Time Stops for No Mouse, Michael Hoeye (Sequel: *The Sands of Time*)

Tuck Everlasting, by Natalie Babbitt (Also: *The Search for Delicious*)

The Watsons Go to Birmingham, by Christopher Paul Curtis (Also: *Bud, Not Buddy*)

When Zachary Beaver Came to Town, by Kimberly Willis Holt

The Whipping Boy, by Sid Fleischman

Windmill Windup, by Matt Christopher (Also: *The Basket Counts, Dirt Bike Racer, Dive Right In, Goalkeeper in Charge, Ice Magic, Return of the Home Run Kid, Tough to Tackle, Wheel Wizards*)

NOVELS FOR OLDER BOYS

The Amazing and Death Defying Diary of Eugene Dingman, by Paul Zindel

Arthur: The Seeing Stone (Trilogy), by Kevin Crossley-Holland

Artemis Fowl, by Eoin Colfer (Sequel: *Artemis Fowl: The Arctic Incident*)

Misery Guts, by Morris Gleitzman (Also: *Blabber Mouth, Two Weeks with the Queen*)

The Boy in the Burning House, by Tim Wynne-Jones (Also: *The Maestro, Stephen Fair*)

California Blue, by David Klass

Camp X, by Eric Walters (Also: *The Bully Boys, Diamonds in the Rough, The Hydrofoil Mystery, Stand Your Ground, Stars, Tiger by the Tail, Trapped in Ice, Visions, War of the Eagles*)

The Contender, by Robert Lipsyte (Also: *The Brave*)

Cowboys Don't Cry, by Marilyn Halvorson (Also: *Cowboys Don't Quit*)

Cyclops, by Clive Cussler (Also: *Inca Gold*)

Dorp Dead, by Julia Cunningham and Betsy Hearne

Dragonwings, by Laurence Yep

Dust, by Arthur Slade (Also: *Tribes*)

A Family Apart, by Joan L. Nixon

Far North, by Will Hobbs (Also: *Down the Yukon, Jason's Gold*)

Feather Boy, by Nicky Singer

Flour Babies, by Anne Fine (Also: *The Diary of a Killer Cat*)

Frozen Fire: A Tale of Courage, by James Houston (Also: *The White Archer, Ice Swords, Long Claws*)

Gentlehands, by M. E. Kerr (Also: *The Books of Fell*)

The Giver, by Lois Lowry (Also: *Gathering Blue*)

The Golden Compass (Trilogy), by Philip Pullman

The Gospel According to Larry, by Janet Tashjian

Hatchet, by Gary Paulsen (Also: *Brian's Return, Brian's Winter, Guts: The True Stories behind* Hatchet *and the Brian Books*)

Julie of the Wolves, by Jean Craighead George (Also: *My Side of the Mountain*)

Killing Mr. Griffin, by Lois Duncan (Also: *I Know What You Did Last Summer, Ransom*)

The Haunting, by Margaret Mahy

The Hobbit, by J. R. R. Tolkien

Hold Fast, by Kevin Major (Also: *Dear Bruce Springsteen, Far from Shore, No Man's Land*)

I Am David, by Anne Holm

I Was a Teenage Professional Wrestler, by Ted Lewin

In Ned's Head, by Soren Olsson and Anders Jacobsson

If Rock and Roll Were a Machine, by Terry Davis

Ironman, by Chris Crutcher (Also: *Athletic Shorts, The Crazy Horse Electric Game, Running Loose, Stotan!, Staying Fat for Sarah Byrnes*)

The Last Book in the Universe, by Rodman Philbrick (Also: *Freak the Mighty, Max the Mighty*)

The Last Mission, by Harry Mazer

The Last Safe Place on Earth, by Richard Peck

A Little Bit of Dead, by Chap Reaver

The Loop, by Nicholas Evans

Lord of the Rings (Trilogy), by J. R. R. Tolkien

The Machine-Gunners, by Robert Westall

Mama's Gonna Buy You a Mockingbird, by Jean Little (Also: *Different Dragons, From Anna, Willow and Twig*)

Maniac Magee, by Jerry Spinelli (Also: *Crash, The Library Card, Space Station Seventh Grade*)

Mary Ann Alice, by Brian Doyle (Also: *Angel Square, Hey Dad!, Spuds Sweetgrass, Up to Low*)

Maus: A Survivor's Tale, by Art Spiegelman

The Maze, by Monica Hughes (Also: *The Dream Catcher, The Golden Aquarians, Invitation to the Game, The Isis Trilogy, Ring-Rise, Ring Set, Sandwriter, The Story Box, The Tomorrow City*)

Monster, by Walter D. Myers (Also: *Fast Sam, Cool Clyde and Stuff, The Mouse Rap, The Outside Shot, Scorpions, Slam!*)

Mrs. Frisby and the Rats of NIMH, by Robert C. O'Brien (Also *Racso and the Rats of NIMH* and *R-T, Margaret, and the Rats of NIMH* by Jane L. Conly)

No More Dead Dogs, by Gordon Korman

Nothing But the Truth, by Avi (Also: *City of Light/City of Dark: A Comic Book Novel, Captain Grey, The Fighting Ground, The Man Who Was Poe, Wolf Rider*)

The Number Devil: A Mathematical Adventure, by Hans Magnus Enzensberger

The Outsiders, by S. E. Hinton (Also: *Rumble Fish, Tex, That Was Then/This Is Now*)

Pacific Crossing, by Gary Soto (Also: *Jesse, Taking Sides*)

Parzival: The Quest of the Grail Knight, by Katherine Paterson (Also: *The Great Gilly Hopkins, Jip: His Story, Preacher's Boy*)

The Rag and Bone Shop, by Robert Cormier (Also: *After the First Death, The Bumblebee Flies Away, The Chocolate War, Heroes, Frenchtown Summer, I Am the Cheese*)

Rainbow Boys, by Alex Sanchez

Reef of Death, by Paul Zindel

Rule of the Bone, by Russell Banks

Sabriel, by Garth Nix (Sequel: *Lirael*)

The Secret Diary of Adrian Mole, Aged 13 (Trilogy), by Sue Townsend

The Shark Callers, by Eric Campbell

The Sight, by David Clement-Davies

Silent to the Bone, by E. L. Konigsburg (Also: *Sunwing, Firewing*)

Silverwing (Trilogy), by Kenneth Oppel

Skellig, by David Almond

Slake's Limbo, by Felice Holman

The Smartest Man in Ireland, by Mollie Hunter (Also: *A Stranger Came Ashore, The Walking Stones*)

The Smugglers (Trilogy), by Iain Lawrence

Soldier's Heart, by Gary Paulsen (Also: *The Beet Fields, The Car, The Cookcamp, Dancing Carl, Dogsong, Harris and Me, The Monument, The Rifle, Sentries, Tracker, The Transall Saga,* The Tucket Adventures (Series), *The Voyage of the Frog, The Winter Room*)

A Solitary Blue, by Cynthia Voight

Son of the Mob, by Gordon Korman

Speak, by Laurie Halse Anderson

Stones, by William Bell (Also: *Crabbe, The Forbidden City, No Signature, Zack*)

Stowaway, by Karen Hesse (Also: *Phoenix Rising*)

Tangerine, by Edward Bloor

The Thief Lord, by Cornelia Funke

Things Not Seen, by Andrew Clements

Thunder Cave, by Roland Smith (Also: *Jaguar*)

Unbelievable!, by Paul Jennings (Also: *Unmentionable!, Totally Wicked!, Come Back Gizmo*)

Walk Two Moons, by Sharon Creech

Seek, by Paul Fleischman (Also: *The Borning Room, Bull Run, Seedfolks, Whirligig*)

The White Mountains (Trilogy), by John Christopher

The Windsinger (Trilogy), by William Nicholson

A Wizard of Earthsea (Trilogy), by Ursula Le Guin

Wringer, by Jerry Spinelli

A Wrinkle in Time (Trilogy), by Madeleine L'Engle

WORD PLAY BOOKS

The Amazing Pop-up Grammar Book, by J. Maizels

A Cache of Jewels and Other Collective Nouns, by Ruth Heller (Also: *Kites Sail High: A Book about Verbs, Many Luscious Lollipops: A Book about Adjectives, Merry-Go-Round: A Book about Nouns*)

A Chocolate Moose for Dinner, by Fred Gwynne (Also: *The King Who Rained, The Sixteen Hand Horse, A Little Pigeon Toad*)

Antics, by Cathi Hepworth

Biggest Riddle Book in the World, by Joseph Rosenbloom

Eight Ate: A Feast of Homonym Riddles, by Marvin Terban (Also: *The Dove Dove: Funny Homograph Riddles, Guppies in Tuxedos: Funny Eponyms, Mad as a Wet Hen and Other Funny Idioms, What's Mite Might? Homophone riddles*)

Feg: Ridiculous Poems for Intelligent Children, by Robin Hirsch

Go Hang a Salami/I'm a Lasagna Hog: And Other Palindromes, by Jon Agee (Also: *So Many Dynamos: And Other Palindromes*)

Green Eggs and Ham, by Dr. Seuss

Ha! Ha! Ha!: 1000 + Jokes, Riddles and Facts, by Lynn Thomas

Jeremy Kooloo, by Tim Mahurin

Kids Are Punny, edited by Rosie O'Donnell

The Napping House, by Audrey Wood (Also: *Piggies, Silly Sally*)

Pass the Celery, Ellery!, by Jeffrey Fisher

Pets in Trumpets and Other Word-Play Riddles, by Bernard Most (Also: *Zoodles*)

Q Is for Duck: An Alphabet Guessing Game, by M. Eltiming

Roadsigns, by Margery Cuyler

Scared Silly: A Book for the Brave: Poems, Riddles, Jokes, Stories and More, by Marc Brown

There's an Ant in Anthony, by Bernard Most

Tomfoolery: Trickery and Foolery with Words, by Alvin Schwartz (Also: *Busy Buzzing Bumblebees and Other Tongue Twisters, The Cat's Elbow and Other Secret Languages, Flapdoodle*)

Tomorrow's Alphabet, by George Shannon

Under, over, by the Clover: What Is a Preposition?, by Brian P. Cleary (Also: *A Mink, a Fink, a Skating Rink: What Is a Noun?, Hairy, Scary, Ordinary: What Is an Adjective?, To Root, to Toot, to Parachute: What Is a Verb?*)

World's Toughest Tongue Twisters, by Jeffrey Rosenbloom

EASY-READ POETRY

A Child's Treasury of Nursery Rhymes, by Kady MacDonald Denton

Bubblegum Delicious, by Dennis Lee (Also: *Jelly Belly, The Ice Cream Store, Alligator Pie, Garbage Delight*)

Eenie Meenie Manitoba, by Robert Heidbreder (Also: *Don't Eat Spiders*)

The Frog Wore Red Suspenders, by Jack Prelutsky (Also: *Ride a Purple Pelican, Beneath a Blue Umbrella*)

Give Yourself to the Rain: Poems for the Very Young, by Margaret Wise Brown

Good for You: Toddler Rhymes for Toddler Times, by Stephanie Calmenson

My Very First Mother Goose, edited by Iona Opie (Also: *Here Comes Mother Goose*)

Read-Aloud Rhymes for the Very Young, edited by Jack Prelutsky

Sports! Sports! Sports!, edited by Lee Bennett Hopkins

There's a Mouse in My House, by Sheree Fitch (Also: *Sleeping Dragons All Around, There Were Monkeys in My Kitchen*)

POETRY FOR YOUNG BOYS

At the Crack of the Bat, edited by Lillian Morrison

The Beauty of the Beast, edited by Jack Prelutsky

Big, Bad and a Little Bit Scary: Poems That Bite Back, edited by Wade Zahares

Blackbird Has Spoken, by Eleanor Farjeon

DeShawn Days, by Tony Medina

Doctor Knickerbocker and Other Rhymes, by David Booth (Also: *Til All the Stars Have Fallen, Images of Nature*)

Doodle Dandies: Poems That Take Shape, by Patrick J. Lewis

Extra Innings: Baseball Poems, edited by Lee Bennett Hopkins

Fearless Fernie, by Gary Soto (Also: *Chato's Kitchen, Chato and the Party Animals, Too Many Tamales, Nerdlandia, Snapshots from the Wedding*)

Footprints on the Roof: Poems about the Earth, by Marilyn Singer (Also: *Monster Museum, Turtle in July*)

For Laughing Out Loud, edited by Jack Prelutsky (Also: *For Laughing Out Louder*)

For the Love of the Game: Michael Jordan and Me, by Eloise Greenfield

Hey You! C'mere: A Poetry Slam, by Elizabeth Swados

It's Raining Pigs and Noodles, by Jack Prelutsky (Also: *The New Kid on the Block, Something Big Has Been Here, A Pizza the Size of the Sun*)

Joyful Noise: Poems for Two Voices, by Paul Fleischman (Also: *I Am Phoenix, Big Talk: Poems For Four Voices*)

Kids Pick the Funniest Poems, edited by Bruce Lansky

The Kingfisher Book of Funny Poems, edited by Roger McGough

Laugh-eteria, by Douglas Florian (Also: *Bing, Bang, Bong*)

Lizards, Frogs and Polliwogs, by Douglas Florian (Also: *Beast Feast, Insectlopedia, In the Swim, On the Wing, Mammalia*)

Love to Langston, by Tony Medina

Lunch Money: And Other Poems about School, by Carol Diggory Shields

Monster Goose, by Judy Sierra

Nathaniel Talking, by Eloise Greenfield

Nothing Beats a Pizza, by Loris Lesynski (Also: *Dirty Dog Boogie*)

Outside the Lines, by Brad Burg and Rebecca Gibbon

A Poke in the Eye: A Collection of Concrete Poems, edited by Paul B. Janeczko

The Random House Book of Poetry, edited by Jack Prelutsky

Relatively Speaking, by Ralph Fletcher

Scary Poems for Rotten Kids, by Sean O'Huigin

Space Time Rhythm and Rhyme, by Russell Stannard

Sports Pages, by Arnold Adoff

Summersaults, by Douglas Florian (Also: *Winter Eyes*)

There's an Awful Lot of Weirdos in Our Neighborhood and Other Wickedly Funny Verse, by Colin McNaughton (Also: *Making Friends with Frankenstein, Who's Been Sleeping in My Porridge?*)

Tomie de Paola's Book of Poems, edited by Tomie de Paola

The 20th Century Children's Poetry Treasury, edited by Jack Prelutsky

Unzip Your Lips: 100 Poems to Read Aloud, by Paul Cookson (Also: *Unzip Your Lips Again*)

Walking the Bridge of Your Nose, edited by Michael Rosen

Where the Sidewalk Ends, by Shel Silverstein (Also: *A Light in the Attic, Falling Up*)

A World of Wonders: Geographic Travels in Verse and Rhyme, by J. Patrick Lewis (Also: *A Burst of Firsts, The Bookworm's Feast*)

Wouldn't You Like to Know, by Michael Rosen

POETRY FOR OLDER BOYS

The Basket Counts, by Arnold Adoff

Carver: A Life in Poems, by Marilyn Nelson

I Feel a Little Jumpy around You: Paired Poems by Men and Women, by Naomi Shihab Nye and Paul B. Janeczko

Girl Coming in for a Landing: A Novel in Poems, by April Halprin Waylind

He Said, She Said, They Said, edited by Anne Harvey

Nightmares: Poems to Trouble Your Sleep, by Jack Prelutsky (Also: *The Headless Horseman Rides Tonight*)

Read Me 1: A Poem for Every Day of the Year, edited by Gaby Morgan (Also: *Read Me 2*)

Remember the Bridge: Poems of a People, by Carole Boston Weatherford

Rimshots, by Charles R. Smith Jr.

The Ring of Words, by Roger McGough

Seeing the Blue Between: Advice and Inspiration for Young Poets, by Paul B. Janeczko (Also: *The Place My Words Are Looking For*)

Words with Wings: A Treasury of African-American Poetry and Art, edited by Belinda Rochelle

NON-FICTION

The Abracadabra Kid: A Writer's Life, by Sid Fleischman

Arthur Ashe: Breaking the Color Barrier, by David Wright

Backfield Package, by Thomas Dygard

Bad Boy: A Memoir, by Walter Dean Myers

Bat, by Caroline Arnold and Richard Hewitt (Also: *Cats in the Wild*)

Boy: Tales of Childhood, by Roald Dahl (Also: *Going Solo*)

Boys Know It All, edited by Michelle Roehm

Boys Who Rocked the World, by Lars de Souza

Caught by the Sea: My Life on Boats, by Gary Paulsen (Also: *Father Water, Mother Woods, Puppie, Dogs, and Blue Northers*)

Chicken Soup for the Teenage Soul, by Jack Canfield and Mark Victor

Children of the Dust Bowl: The True Story of the Weedpatch Camp, by Jerry Stanley

China Boy, by Gus Lee

Dinosaurs! The Biggest, Baddest, Strangest, Fastest, by Howard Zimmerman

Disasters! Catastrophes That Shook the World, by Richard Bonson and Richard Platt

Eyewitness Books (Series)

Fire in Their Eyes: Wildfires and the People Who Fight Them, by Karen Magnuson Beil

The 5,000-Year-Old Puzzle: Solving a Mystery of Ancient Egypt, by Claudia Logan

Flying to the Moon: An Astronaut's Story, by Michael Collins

Frederick Douglass: The Last Day of Slavery, by William Miller

Gandhi, by Leonard Everet Fisher

The Grapes of Math, by Greg Tang (Also: *Math for All Seasons*)

The Greatest: Muhammad Ali, by Walter Dean Myers

The Greatest Goal, by Mike Leonetti

Guinness World Records 2002

Hockey for Kids: Heroes, Tips and Facts, by Brian McFarlane

A Hope in the Unseen: An American Odyssey from the Inner City to the Ivy League, by Ron Suskind

How Things Work, by David Macaulay (Also: *Building Big, Castle, City, Pyramid, Unbuilding, Underground*)

How Hockey Works, by Keltie Thomas

I Spy (Series), by Jean Marzollo

If the World Were a Village, by David J. Smith

In Flanders Fields: The Story of the Poem by John McCrae, by Linda Granfield

Knots in My Yo-Yo String: The Autobiography of a Kid, by Jerry Spinelli

The Librarian Who Measured the Earth, by Kathryn Lasky

The Magic School Bus (Series), by Joanna Cole

The Man Who Ran Faster Than Anyone: The Story of Tom Longboat, by Jack Batten

Mark Twain: America's Humorist, Dreamer, Prophet, by Clinton Cox

Martin's Big Words, by Doreen Rappaport

Michael Jordan: Basketball Great, by Sean Dolan

The Most Amazing Science Pop-up Book, by Jay Young

Nelson Mandela: Voice of Freedom, by Libby Hughes

No More! Stories and Songs of Slave Resistance, by Doreen Rappaport

Pier 21: Gateway of Hope, by Linda Granfield (Also: *97 Orchard Street, New York*)

A Puzzling Day in the Land of the Pharaohs: A Search-and-Solve Gamebook, by Scoular Anderson

Red Leaf, Yellow Leaf, by Lois Ehlert

Still Me, by Christopher Reeve

Rocket Boys: A Memoir, by Homer Hickman Jr.

Super String Games, by Camilla Gryski

The Tall Mexican: The Life of Hang Aguirre All-Star Pitcher, Businessman, Humanitarian, by Robert Copley

The Tarantula in My Purse and 172 Other Wild Pets, by Jean Craighead George

Tea That Burns: A Family Memoir of Chinatown, by Bruce Edward Hall

Too Young to Fight: Memories from Youth from World War II, by Priscilla Galloway

The World Almanac for Kids

Z Is for Zamboni: A Hockey Alphabet, by Mike Ulmer (Also: *M Is for Maple*)

Professional Reading

A conversation with literary critic Harold Bloom. (2001, May). *Harvard Business Review, 79* (5), 63–68.

Allen, J. (1999). *Words, words, words: Teaching vocabulary in grades 4–12*. Portland, ME: Stenhouse.

Anderson, C. (2000). *How's it going?* Portsmouth, NH: Heinemann.

Anderson, L. H. (1999). *Speak*. New York: Farrar Straus Giroux.

Bannert, M., & Arbinger, P. R. (1996, September). Gender-related differences in exposure to and use of computers: Results of a survey of secondary school students. *European Journal of Psychology of Education, 11* (3), 269–282.

Barrs, M., & Cork, V. (2001). *The reader in the writer: The links between the study of literature and writing development at key stage 2*. London: Centre for Language in Primary Education.

Barrs, M., & Pidgeon, S. (Eds.). (1998). *Boys & reading*. London: Centre for Language in Primary Education (LB Southwark).

Barrs, M., & Pidgeon, S. (Eds.). (1994). *Reading the difference: Gender and reading in elementary classrooms*. Markham, ON: Pembroke.

Belenky, M. F. (1986). *Women's ways of knowing: The development of self, voice, and mind*. New York: Basic Books.

Bomer, R. (1995). *Time for meaning*. Portsmouth, NH: Heinemann.

Booth, D. (2001). *Reading & writing in the middle years*. Markham, ON: Pembroke/Portland, ME: Stenhouse.

Booth, D. (1998). *Guiding the reading process: Techniques and strategies for successful instruction in K–8 classrooms*. Markham, ON: Pembroke/Portland, ME: Stenhouse.

Booth, D. (1994). *Classroom voices: Language-based learning in the elementary school*. Toronto: Harcourt Brace.

Booth, D. (1994). *Story drama: Reading, writing and roleplaying across the curriculum*. Markham, ON: Pembroke.

Booth, D., & Barton, R. (2001). *Story works*. Markham, ON: Pembroke.

Bouchard, D. (2001). *The gift of reading*. Victoria, BC: Orca.

Bourne, P., McCoy, L., & Novogrodsky, M. (Eds.). (1997). Gender and schooling. *Orbit, 28* (1).

Brozo, W. G. (2002). *To be a boy, to be a reader: Engaging teen and preteen boys in active literacy*. Newark, DE: International Reading Association.

Calkins, L. (2001). *The art of teaching reading*. New York: Addison-Wesley.

Coles, R. (1990). *The spiritual life of children*. Boston, MA: Houghton Mifflin.

Cunningham, P., et al. (1995). *Reading & writing in elementary classrooms*. White Plains, NY: Longman.

Dorn, L. J., & Soffos, C. (2001). *Shaping literate minds: Developing self-regulated learners*. Portland, ME: Stenhouse.

Egendorf, L. K. (Ed.). (2000). *Male/female roles: Opposing viewpoints*. San Diego, CA: Greenhaven Press.

Eisler, R. (2000). *Tomorrow's children: A blueprint for partnership education in the 21st century*. Boulder, CO: Westview Press.

Faludi, S. (1999). *Stiffed: The betrayal of the American man*. New York: Perennial.

Feinburg, S. G. (1979). The significance of what boys and girls choose to draw: Explorations of fighting and helping. In J. Loeb (Ed.), *Feminist collage: Educating women in the visual arts* (pp. 185–196). New York: Teachers College Press.

Fletcher, R. (1993). *What a writer needs*. Portsmouth, NH: Heinemann.

Fletcher, R., & Portalupi, J. (1998). *Craft lessons: Teaching writing K–8*. Portland, ME: Stenhouse.

Fountas, I. C., & Pinnell, G. S. (2001). *Guiding readers and writers*. Portsmouth, NH: Heinemann.

Fountas, I., & Pinnell, G. S. (Eds.). (1999). *Voices on word matters: Learning about phonics and spelling in the literacy classroom*. Portsmouth, NH: Heinemann.

Fountas, I. C., & Pinnell, G. S. (1996). *Guided reading*. Portsmouth, NH: Heinemann.

Gallagher, K. (2000). *Drama education in the lives of girls: Imagining possibilities*. Toronto: University of Toronto Press.

Garbarino, James, & Ellen de Lara. (2002). *And words can hurt forever: How to protect adolescents from bullying, harassment and emotional violence.* New York: The Free Press.

Gilbert, S. (2000). *A field guide to boys and girls.* New York: HarperCollins.

Goleman, D. (1998). *Working with emotional intelligence.* New York: Bantam Books.

Gurian, M. (1998). *A fine young man: What parents, mentors, and educators can do to shape adolescent boys into exceptional men.* New York: Jeremy P. Tarcher/Putnam.

Gurian, M. (1996). *The wonder of boys: What parents, mentors and educators can do to shape boys into exceptional men.* New York: Jeremy P. Tarcher/Putnam.

Gurian, M., & Henley, P. (2001). *Boys and girls learn differently: A guide for teachers and parents.* San Francisco: Jossey-Bass.

Hall, C., & Coles, M. (1997). Gendered readings: Helping boys develop as critical readers. *Gender and Education, 9* (1), 61–68.

Hartley, J. (2001). *Reading groups.* New York: Oxford University Press.

Harvey, S. (1998). *Nonfiction matters: Reading, writing, and research in grades 3–8.* York, ME: Stenhouse.

Harvey, S., & Goudvis, A. (2000). *Strategies that work: Teaching comprehension to enhance understanding.* Portland, ME: Stenhouse.

Harwayne, S. (2000). *Lifetime guarantees: Toward ambitious literacy teaching.* Portsmouth, NH: Heinemann.

Huber, B., & Schofield, J. W. (1998). "I like computers, but many girls don't": Gender and the sociocultural context of computing. In H. Bromley & M. H. Apple (Eds.), *Education/technology/power: Educational computing as a social practice* (pp. 103–132). Albany: State University of New York Press.

Janeczko, P. B. (Ed.). (2002). *Seeing the blue between: Advice and inspiration for young poets.* Cambridge, MA: Candlewick Press.

Jobe, R., & Dayton-Sakari, M. (2002). *Info-kids: How to use nonfiction to turn reluctant readers into enthusiastic learners.* Markham, ON: Pembroke.

Jobe, R., & Dayton-Sakari, M. (1999). *Reluctant readers: Connecting students and books for successful reading experiences.* Markham, ON: Pembroke.

King, Stephen. (2000). *On writing: A memoir of the craft.* New York: Scribner.

Kivel, Paul. (1999). *Boys will be men.* Gabriola Island, BC: New Society Publishers.

Klein, N. (2000). *No LOGO: Taking aim at the brand bullies.* Toronto: Vintage Canada.

Kohn, A. (1999). *The schools our children deserve: Moving beyond traditional classrooms and "together standards."* New York: Houghton Mifflin.

Kohn, A. (1993) *Punished by Rewards.* Boston: Houghton Mifflin.

Lamott, A. (1994). *Bird by bird: Some instructions on writing and life.* New York: Anchor Books.

Lanius, C. (1999). *Getting girls interested in technology.* Texas: Rice University.

Leu, D. J., Jr., & Leu, D. D. (1997). *Teaching with the Internet: Lessons from the classroom.* Norwood, MA: Christopher-Gordon Publishers.

Livingstone, Margaret, & Hubel, David H. (2002) *Vision and Art: The Biology of Seeing.* New York: Harry N. Abrams.

Majewski, M. M. (1979). Female art characteristics: Do they really exist? In J. Loeb (Ed.), *Feminist collage: Educating women in the visual arts* (pp. 197–200). New York: Teachers College Press.

Martin, J. (2002, June). Listen up. *Men's Health, 17* (5), 81.

Mason, J. (2001, July 20). Growing vegetables and shooting hoops. *The Globe and Mail,* p. A16.

Mearns, H. (1958). *Creative power: The education of youth in the creative arts* (2nd Rev. ed.). New York: Dover Publications.

Millard, E. (1997). *Differently literate: Boys, girls and the schooling of literacy.* Washington, DC: Falmer Press.

Minns, H. (1991). *Language, literacy & gender.* London: Hodder & Stoughton

Moline, S. (1995). *I see what you mean: Children at work with visual information.* Portland, ME: Stenhouse/Markham, ON: Pembroke.

Moloney, J. (2000). *Boys and books: Building a culture of reading around our boys.* Sydney, NSW: ABC Books.

Newberger, E. H. (1999). *The men they will become: The nature and nurture of male character.* Reading, MA: Perseus Books.

Newkirk, T. (2000, March). Misreading masculinity: Speculations on the great gender gap in writing. *Language Arts, 77* (4), 294–300.

Nye, N. S., & Janeczko, P. B. (Eds.). (1996). *I feel a little jumpy around you: Paired poems by men & women.* New York: Aladdin Paperbacks.

Pennac, D. (1994). *Better than life.* (D. Homel, Trans.) Markham, ON: Pembroke/Portland, ME: Stenhouse.

Philbrick, R. (2000). *The last book in the universe.* New York: Blue Sky Press.

Pike, M. A. (2000, Autumn). Boys, poetry and the individual talent. *English in Education, 34* (3), 41–55.

Pinker, S. (1994). *The language instinct.* New York: HarperPerennial.

Pinnell, G. S., & Fountas, I. C. (1998). *Word matters: Teaching phonics and spelling in the reading/writing classroom.* Portsmouth, NH: Heinemann.

Polce-Lynch, M. (2002). *Boy talk.* Oakland, CA: New Harbinger Publications.

Pollack, W. S. (2000). *Real boys' voices.* New York: Penguin Books.

Pollack, W. S., & Cushman, K. (2001). *Real boys workbook.* New York: Villard.

Postman, N. (1995). *The end of education: Redefining the value of school.* New York: Vintage Books.

Rosen, B. (1988). *And none of it was nonsense: The power of storytelling in school.* Richmond Hill, ON: Scholastic.

Rosen, B. (1991). *Shapers and polishers: Teachers as storytellers.* London: Mary Glasgow Publications.

Routman, R. (2000). *Conversations.* Portsmouth, NH: Heinemann.

Rowan, L., Knobel, M., Bigum, C., & Lankshear, C. (2002). *Boys, literacies and schooling: The dangerous territories of gender-based literacy reform.* Buckingham, UK: Open University Press.

Sabin, R. (1996). *Comics, comix & graphic novels: A history of comic art.* London: Phaidon Press.

Saric, Julia. (2001). A defense of Potter, or when religion is not religion: An analysis of the censoring of the Harry Potter books. *Canadian Children's Literature, 27*(3), 6–26.

Severiens, S. E., & Dam, G. T. M. (1994, June). Gender differences in learning styles: A narrative review and quantitative meta-analysis. *Higher Education, 27* (4), 487–501.

Smith, M. W., & Wilhelm, J. D. (2002). *"Reading don't fix no Chevys": Literacy in the lives of young men.* Portsmouth, NH: Heinemann.

Stead, T. (2002). *Is that a fact? Teaching nonfiction writing K–3.* Portland, ME: Stenhouse.

Strickland, D. S., Ganske, K., & Monroe, J. K. (2002). *Supporting struggling readers and writers: Strategies for classroom intervention 3–6.* Portland, ME: Stenhouse.

Swartz, L. (1993). *Classroom events through poetry.* Markham, ON: Pembroke.

Tovani, C. (2000). *I read it, but I don't get it: Comprehension strategies for adolescent readers.* Portland, ME: Stenhouse.

Volman, M., & Eck, E. V. (2001, Winter). Gender equity and information technology in education: The second decade. *Review of Educational Research, 71* (4), 613–634.

Weaver, S. (2001). *Teenage boys talk: 50 New Zealand teenagers talk about their lives.* Glenfield, Auckland: Random House New Zealand.

Wells, G., & Chang-Wells, G. L. (1992). *Constructing knowledge together: Classrooms as centers of inquiry and literacy.* Portsmouth, NH: Heinemann.

Willingham, W. W., & Johnson, L. M. (Eds.). (1997, May). *Supplement to gender and fair assessment* (ETS RR-97-1). Princeton, NJ: Educational Testing Service.

Witt, S. D. (2001). The influence of school texts on children's gender role socialization. *Curriculum and Teaching, 16* (1), 25–43.

Wormeli, R. (2001). *Meet me in the middle: Becoming an accomplished middle-level teacher.* Portland, ME: Stenhouse.

Acknowledgments

I want to thank the teachers who provided such significant interviews and observations on the reading lives of boys and men:

Angela Zezza	Emily Curatolo
Diane Quick	Joanne Saragosa
Duane Heide	Kaia Stahl
Ed VanSloten	Mary Martin
J. Carol Howard	Michelle Kubeka
Lara Teliatnik	Patricia Hektor
Daniela Bascunan	Maureen Cassidy
David Moscinski	Sarah Kochhar
Jim Stathopoulos	Eddie Ing

I want to acknowledge the following friends for their encouragement and support in developing the ideas and strategies for this book:

- Kathleen Gallagher, who bravely carries on a continuing dialogue with me on gender issues;
- Diva Anderson, who added invaluable research on boys and education;
- Shelley Peterson, who is on the cutting edge of literacy concerns;
- Clare Kosnik, who continues to include me in her work in education;
- Kathy Broad, for summarizing the new developments on the brain research;
- Jennifer Rowsell, for her awareness of IT and the effects on children;
- Michael Rossetti, for his powerful literacy work with adolescents;
- Jim Giles, for his continuing efforts at connecting home and school;
- Carol Hennessy, for her coordinating role with the preservice interviews;
- Michael Ross, for his sharing of such wonderful life stories;
- Nancy Steele, for being an amazing classroom teacher;
- Steve Venright, for his poetic words and pictures;
- Jeannie Wilson, for sharing findings from her own research;
- Julia Saric, for her knowledge of the history of books for boys;
- Michael Hurry, for his 25 years of service for the Big Brothers Association as executive director in Sarnia/Lambton;
- Masayuki Hachiya, for his commitment and dedication to this project; and
- Larry Swartz, for his research and assistance in constructing the bibliography for boys.

Index